INSIDE THE BUYER'S BRAIN

How to Turn Buyers into Believers

"Packed with original research, *Inside the Buyer's Brain* shows you what buyers really care about so you can effectively communicate and grow your business."

DAVID MEERMAN SCOTT, bestselling author of *The New Rules of Marketing and PR*

"A *tour de force*... Clearly written and illustrated, this is no-nonsense essential reading for anyone wanting to listen to their customers more closely and align their services accordingly."

JAMES BESWICK, author of *Ranking Number One* and founder of One Uproar

"Everyone says they're client focused in professional services. If you're really client focused, you need to read *Inside the Buyers Brain*."

MIKE SCHULTZ, President, RAIN Group and co-author of *Rainmaking Conversations*

"With deep research and wit, *Inside the Buyer's Brain* illustrates the disconnect between sellers' assumptions and buyers' needs. The more certain you are that you know what matters to your buyers, the more you need to read this book."

IAN ALTMAN, author of *Upside Down Selling* and *Same Side Selling*

"Professional services rainmakers and marketers will gain real insights into the thought processes and values of their target buyers by reading this book! I especially appreciated the new research, the easy-to-digest format and the 10 factors that winners address differently to sell and create ongoing satisfaction. A great read!"

JENNIFER WILSON, Co-founder and Partner, ConvergenceCoaching, LLC

"This timely book should become the bible of professional services firms looking to understand how buyers buy their services — and why they sometimes go to the competition."

NICK MORGAN, author of *Give Your Speech*, Change the World and founder of Public Words

"Inside the Buyer's Brain offers sound research, useful best practices and a pragmatic voice to help get a rainmaker started and to grow their practice."

ANDREW J. SHERMAN, Partner, Jones Day and author of 25 books on business growth and strategic planning, including the best-selling *Harvesting Intangible Assets*

"This is the definitive guide for making deep connections with your customers and establishing building buyer loyalty."

"A novel and effective approach to connecting with your market and closing the sale. This guide shows you the most effective strategies for marketing and developing your professional services business."

MICHAEL FLEISCHNER, President, Upward SEO and author of *SEO Made Simple* *(3rd Edition)*

"A breakthrough book for professional service firms. It turns the challenge of winning business on its head by asking simply 'what do clients want'? The authors expose a chasm in perception between what clients want and what sellers think they need. I can't recommend it highly enough."

SONJA JEFFERSON, Founder of Valuable Content Ltd

Published by Hinge Research Institute

12030 Sunrise Valley Drive, Suite 120
Reston, Virginia 20191

ISBN 978-0-9828819-6-5

Printed in the United States of America

Design by Hinge.

Visit our website at www.hingemarketing.com

INSIDE THE BUYER'S BRAIN

How to Turn Buyers into Believers

Lee W. Frederiksen, Ph.D., Elizabeth Harr,
Sylvia Montgomery, CPSM and Aaron E. Taylor

CONTENTS

ACKNOWLEDGMENTS

It takes an entire team to write and produce a book. We'd like to take this opportunity to appreciate and applaud their efforts.

Research lies at the foundation of this book, so we offer our thanks to Candace Frederiksen who led our team of interviewers, as well as Sean McVey who conducted many of the interviews for the book's case studies. Alexandra Marigodova provided much of the data analysis that inspired this book in the first place.

For their ongoing editorial assistance and writing support, we would like to recognize the tireless work of Eric Gregory, Emily Paterson and John DiConsiglio.

In addition, we'd like to thank our talented design team: Brian Lemen designed the book layout and cover, and he prepared the numerous print and electronic formats. Andrea Kuchinski created the book's attractive and easy-to-read charts.

Of course, we could not have produced this book without the active involvement of our hundreds of research participants. At some level this is their story. Finally, we would like to give a special thanks to the organizations we interviewed as case studies for this book. We hope that their successes will inspire other firms to buck tradition and try a bold, new approach to marketing.

INTRODUCTION

If you are a professional services firm executive interested in growing your business, entering new markets or introducing a new service, you need to get inside the minds of your clients and look at your firm from their perspective. You see, most new business opportunities fail because sellers (like you) make misguided assumptions about the people and companies that buy their services. Whether you know it or not, these folks think differently. And if you want to truly connect with them you need to understand the way their minds work.

This book is here to help.

Using a significant new body of independent research, we uncovered what motivates and de-motivates buyers. But that doesn't tell the whole story. We also needed to understand how sellers expect buyers to behave, so we looked at both sides of the professional services transaction.

Our findings may surprise you. Buyers and sellers experience the marketplace very differently and they often expect different things from their counterparts. Firms that recognize these gaps and take measures to close them have much better odds of winning the business.

We'll take you on an incredible journey inside the buyer's head where you will see these gaps for yourself and learn how to bridge them. Along the way, we'll teach you what it takes to close the sale, build buyer loyalty and encourage more referrals.

Finally, we will explain why your brand is the key to engaging your clients. And we will map out a strategy to build your firm's reputation and make it better known in the marketplace.

So let's head inside!

PART I:
Looking Inside the Buyer's Brain

What you don't know can hurt you.

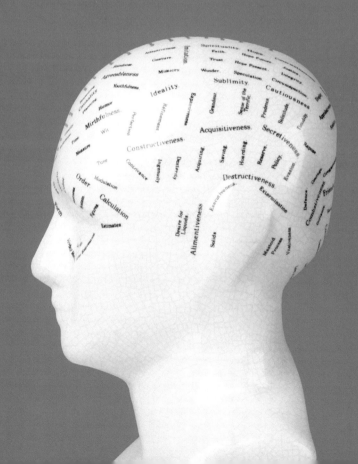

CHAPTER 1
Buyers vs. Sellers

R unning a professional services firm isn't easy — coordinating multiple complex projects, meeting deadlines and managing staff are hard enough. But for many firms, producing a steady stream of new clients can be an even tougher nut to crack.

You see, buyers of professional services can be fickle and frustrating. At their worst, prospective clients are unpredictable, nearly impossible to please and slow to select a firm. At their best, they can close in a New York minute. Most, of course, fall somewhere in-between. With such a wide range of behaviors, buyers' psychology appears to be all over the map.

Our previous research on professional services firms showed that high growth, high profit firms have a strong understanding of their target clients. The more they know about their clients, the faster they grow.

So what makes buyers tick? What do they want? Why can't they see what's obvious to you—that your firm is an exceptional fit and a good value? Is there anything you can do to make the process easier for you and your prospective clients?

We just had to find out.

A Head for Research

We don't just do research for the fun of it. (Though it *is* fun.) Again and again, we've noticed that firms with high growth and high profits conduct regular research on their target clients.

Figure 1.1. The Impact of Research on Firm Growth and Profitability

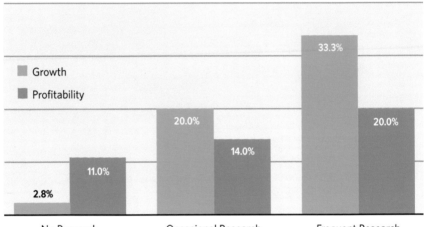

As Figure 1.1 illustrates, firms that do frequent research (at least once per quarter) on target clients outperform firms that do occasional research (less than once per quarter) or none at all. Research is rewarding — and we wanted to bring these rewards to firms that aren't at all sure what's going on inside clients' heads.

So we rolled up our sleeves and launched a study of over 1,300 buyers and sellers of professional services. In this study, we set out to understand why the relationship between the two sides is so, well ... awkward. And we hoped to uncover a way to help professional services firms reduce the friction between buyers and sellers. If we could diagnose the problem, we'd have a good chance of finding an effective solution.

Using a combination of phone interviews and online surveys, we gathered the perspectives of professional services marketers and buyers. We also reviewed findings from RAIN Group, who conducted a simultaneous, cooperative study of over 700 business-to-business (B2B) sales opportunities.

> What we found was an utter failure to see the marketplace in the same way.

After we had collected all the data and analyzed the numbers we discovered an interesting trend. At key points in the buyer-seller relationship we noticed substantial gaps between the way the two sides perceived and understood key issues.

Buyers and Sellers: Brains Divided
There was no ignoring the gaps. It was as if buyers and sellers were using opposite sides of their brains. Where one would see strength, the other would see weakness. Where one would value specific traits or skills, the other would value entirely different things. What we found was more than a breakdown in communication. It was an utter failure to see the marketplace in the same way.

In fact, our findings got us pretty excited. If we could identify where sellers were misreading buyers, we could give firms the inside information they need to communicate their messages more efficiently and close more business. They could adjust their strategy — and their brand — to match the expectations of their buyers. Buyers would recognize a good fit and value sooner. And sellers would close more business and be able to grow faster. Powerful stuff!

One Story, Two Readings

Inside the Seller's Brain

Daniel couldn't believe it. This morning, he opened the business section of his newspaper and read a story that took him by surprise. His IT firm's most loyal client had just inked a large contract with a competitor. In fact, this competitor didn't have half the experience his firm did in the technology they were hired to upgrade. To make matters worse, his firm — a respected, regional technology integrator — had never even been asked to bid.

His firm was just wrapping up a complex two-year project in which they had designed and installed a new check processing system and integrated it with the client's legacy accounting system. This type of project can easily go awry, yet in this case they had nailed every milestone and the new system would go online ahead of schedule.

On more than one occasion, Daniel's point of contact, Maxine, had told them what a great job they had done. And she'd even said her company would hire them again when the project's next phase kicked in next year.

So what gives? Why didn't they even consider Daniel's firm for the new IT project? More than a little peeved, he dialed her number.

Inside the Buyer's Brain
When Maxine received Daniel's call at 9:30 am, she had just gotten off the phone with her company's new IT security partner. She hoped this was the beginning of the end of a stressful five-week period. The network she oversaw had been compromised not once, but three times, by malicious attacks. Only her department's nightly backups had saved the company — and Maxine's job — from disaster.

Daniel skipped the pleasantries. "I saw in the paper that you hired Firm X to handle your IT security. I don't get it. I've gotten nothing but positive feedback from you. Did we do something wrong?"

Maybe it was her lack of sleep, but Maxine was confused. "I don't understand, Daniel. Your team did a fantastic job. I've told you that."

"Then why weren't we allowed to bid on the security job?"

"I may not have mentioned it to you," she said, "but one of our systems had been badly hacked. We needed a specialist who could fix the problem for good."

"But we've helped a lot companies deal with exactly the same problem. And some of those companies are a lot bigger than you. It's plain as day on our website!"

Maxine went on to explain that she had hired Daniel's firm to solve a specific problem — integrating a new check processing system into their accounting system. Because a friend in the industry had referred Daniel's firm, she hadn't spent a lot of time going over their list of services (and even if she had, she probably wouldn't have remembered). Daniel's firm had done the job so well, in fact, that she assumed they worked primarily with accounting systems. It had never occurred to her that they had IT security expertise, as well. If she only had known, she would have considered Daniel's firm. But frankly, she has a lot of confidence in the firm she just hired.

Assumption Junction
Daniel and Maxine suffer from the same condition: assumption-itis. On the one hand, Daniel assumed that his client fully understood his firm and what they do. After all, they had been working together for almost two years. On the other hand, Maxine assumed that Daniel's firm does only one thing well — work with accounting systems — because that's the only experience she had with them.

It's not reasonable to expect the buyer to keep abreast of their vendors' capabilities. So it's up to the seller to educate the client about their services.

Now, while both sides could be blamed for the misunderstanding that kept Daniel's firm out of consideration, it's important to understand that only the seller is in a position to do anything about it. After all, it's not reasonable to expect the buyer to keep abreast of its vendors' capabilities. So it's up to the seller to educate the client about its services.

Maxine makes one other important assumption. She hired Firm X because they specialize in IT security. She assumed that because they specialize, they are superior at what they do. We'll return to this issue again in the next chapter.

Mind the Gaps
Daniel and Maxine's misunderstanding isn't unusual. In fact, there are a whole host of perception gaps that can affect the fortunes of a professional services firm. The research that went into this book uncovered many critical areas where buyers and sellers fail to see each other or the marketplace the same way.

Let's take a quick look at some of the gaps that keep many firms from performing at their potential:

- Sellers misunderstand buyers' challenges, so they don't bring the right mix of services to the table.

- Sellers overestimate the importance of their services, so they do a poor job of explaining why their services are relevant to solving a client's problem.

- Sellers are dismissive of many firms that buyers consider their competition. As a result, sellers discount firms they don't think are in their league or that offer different kinds of solutions.

- Buyers value a firm's reputation for producing results much more than sellers think. So sellers that don't consciously develop their reputations will be at a disadvantage.

- Sellers believe cost is a critical driver in the selection process. Many buyers do not.

Clearly, these gaps present perils for the unsuspecting professional services firm. At the same time, however, they offer tremendous opportunities to those who understand what goes on inside the buyer's brain. If you can adjust your marketing approach to meet buyers' expectations, you will be well prepared to win their hearts ... and minds.

Sellers are dismissive of many firms that buyers consider their competition.

In Part II of this book, we will look at these gaps in more detail and suggest ways to close them. But there is even more to learn about buyers. In the next chapter, we'll probe a little deeper into the minds of buyers and begin to discover what it takes to win their confidence, grow the relationship and turn clients into reliable referral sources.

Key Takeaways

- Research has uncovered significant gaps between how buyers and sellers perceive each other and the marketplace.

- Firms that aren't aware of these gaps are much more likely to waste resources and miss valuable opportunities — in short, they are less competitive.

- It is the seller's job to bridge these gaps.

- If you can adjust your marketing to fit buyers' expectations, you will be far more successful.

CHAPTER 2

Turning Buyers into Believers

B uyers' brains are no different than yours or ours. But their experiences in the marketplace, making tough choices with incomplete information, often compel them to approach transactions with caution. Some buyers have been burned in the past. Or they don't want to overspend needlessly. Many don't know how to choose among a large pool of providers. And usually, they aren't qualified to discern the technical differences between the firms they are considering. They're in a tough place.

If you want to connect with your buyers, the first thing you should do is sympathize with their plight. Once you are able to see the bind they are in you'll understand that buyers aren't the only ones with leverage.

You see, you have the power to help buyers choose you.

In the last chapter we looked inside buyers' heads and discovered that they have very different expectations than you do. That's useful information. The gaps that separate buyers and sellers are also opportunities. In fact, most of your competitors stumble into these gaps time and time again because they can't see them. But once you know they are there, you can make adjustments to your marketing to meet those expectations. That will make your firm a lot more savvy — and appealing to your audience.

But there's more to winning than being steady on your feet. You also have to take command of the relationship.

You have to take command of the relationship.

A Little Education Goes a Long Way

If sellers like you are stumbling around the marketplace in the dark, most buyers are right there with you. Most of them don't have the knowledge to hire the professional services firms that are best for them.

They need help. They could really use a guru, a swami, a Jedi master to lead them to the light. If you choose to take on that role, you will be richly rewarded.

Here's how it works. Firms that "teach" take on a special status in the eyes of their students. When your firm produces a wealth of practical, educational materials in your area of expertise, the people who read it (assuming it's accessible and of sufficient quality) begin to trust and rely on you. And when they realize they don't have the time or resources to do the work themselves, guess whose firm they will put at the top of their list of service providers? That's right. Yours.

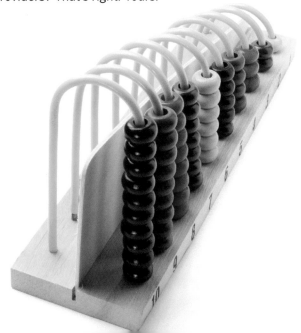

This approach is called *content marketing* and it is changing the way professional services are bought and sold. We describe content marketing in more detail in Chapters 5 and 6.

Ingredients of Winning
What does it take to win in a competitive environment? It's one thing to make the short list; it's quite another to take the prize. So we asked buyers what factors tipped the scale in favor of one firm over another. The results were startling. The winners wooed clients in a very different way than firms that came in second place. What's their secret?

You'll get the whole scoop in Chapter 6. In the meantime, here's a sneak peek: Winners aren't satisfied with presenting their credentials (though these are usually excellent). Instead, they pursue a different strategy. They work hard to gain the trust and confidence of their prospects, offering people a preview of what it's like to work with them. They do this by educating, collaborating with and persuading their prospects. Not surprisingly, this gives them a tremendous advantage against firms that simply respond to a request for proposal (RFP).

After You Close the Sale
Congratulations — you've made the sale! But if you want to get the most out of your client relationship, including additional work and referrals, you have more work to do. You need to keep the client happy so that they will spread the good word about your firm and make referrals.

> Content marketing is changing the way professional services are bought and sold.

That means understanding what they really value in the relationship so that you can deliver not only the appropriate services, but the right messages, too. Remember, most clients aren't competent to evaluate the quality of your services, so they need other assurances that you are doing excellent work.

One thing they look for is a firm that keeps its promises. So set realistic expectations and don't overpromise! And firms that look beyond the task at hand and suggest solutions that address more fundamental problems are often rewarded with additional work and a lot of respect.

You also need to make sure your client is aware of the range of services you provide or you may miss out on some golden opportunities to expand the relationship. If clients don't know what you do, they will hire other firms to do some of those things — no matter how happy they are with you.

In Chapters 7 and 8, we'll dive deeper into these issues and offer some strategies you can use to build stronger ties to your clients.

Getting the Almighty Referral

Winning new clients is great. But winning new clients that refer other clients is golden. Not surprisingly, our research shows that referrals are the number one way that buyers discover service providers. And even as online search becomes an important tool for buyers, referrals aren't going to lose their lead any time soon.

Firms that carve out a place for themselves in the marketplace find it easier to communicate their value proposition and grow.

What can you do to encourage more referrals and grow you business? We just talked about one way — delight your clients. Barely satisfied and unhappy clients aren't going to be a reliable source of praise. And if you have enough of them, they will be a drag on your reputation. In Chapter 9, we outline some ways you can encourage prospects to ask your clients about you. Strategies include publishing case studies about your clients, listing your clients on your website (so that others can see the types of firms you work with) and using public relations to spread the word. Which brings us to one of the most important things your firm can do to build a healthy stream of referrals.

Strengthening Your Brand
In Part III of this book we lay out a program to build a stronger brand that will make generating new business much easier. Having a strong brand makes everything easier — from getting on prospects' lists of candidate firms to closing the sale to lubricating the referral process.

Understanding Your Brand
But what exactly is a brand, anyway? A professional services brand can be defined many ways, but when you boil it down

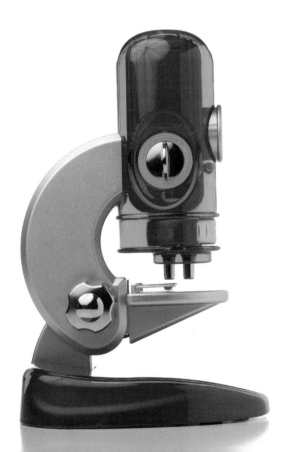

to its essence you are left with two elements: reputation and visibility. You can express these factors in a simple equation:

$$Brand = Reputation \times Visibility$$

You can't have a strong brand without addressing both of these dimensions. Many firms we've worked with, for instance, have strong reputations in small markets. Even though these companies fare well against their local competitors, their brands are relatively weak compared to firms that have national or international exposure. Our research and experience tell us that visibility is one the biggest challenges facing firms that want to grow and compete on a larger stage. To get there, they need a brand that fits the bill.

In Chapters 10 to 13, we lay out a process to retool your firm's brand and make it more relevant to the clientele you serve. We discuss some keys to building a stronger brand that will improve your reputation and provide a foundation for improved visibility in the marketplace. If you can't wait that long to find out what they are, here are a few of the top tactics to strengthen your brand.

Conduct Research
Firms that make the effort to understand their audience's changing needs over time are more likely to experience higher growth and profitability. Conducting research on clients and prospects is the best way to uncover what issues are most relevant to them and how your firm can best help them. It gives you the foundation you need to get the strategy right.

Position Your Firm for Growth

Firms that carve out a place for themselves in the marketplace find it easier to communicate their value proposition and grow. Often this positioning includes taking on a specialty (for example, a particular service line or industry). Specialization helps potential clients quickly grasp which firms are well suited to solve their problem (remember Maxine from chapter 1?). Generalists and firms that don't talk about themselves in a unique way have a tougher time competing against well-positioned firms.

> The better you understand your audience and are able to close the perception gaps that hold your firm back, the more potential you have to grow and prosper.

Develop Brand Tools that Communicate Your Credibility

Your brand and marketing tools offer clues about your firm's credibility. Everything from your logo to your website to your sales collateral should convey a unified message and reflect the best aspects of your brand. If your tools aren't up to snuff, buyers may assume your services reflect a similar inattention to detail.

Taking a Plan to Your Brand

Brand building is an ongoing process. If you want grow your reputation and increase your exposure in the marketplace you will need a thoughtful plan to improve your reputation and visibility — and the discipline to carry it out. In Chapters 12 and 13 we outline such a plan and offer some advice that will help you allocate money and resources to the right activities.

We recommend that you invest in both online marketing and any traditional tactics that are still bearing fruit. If you want to become a recognized thought leader and create a self-seeding mechanism to spread the word, content should become a major focus of your marketing. And you will need to build a high performance website that generates leads and houses your valuable content.

The better you understand your audience and are able to close the perception gaps that hold your firm back, the more potential you have to grow and prosper. We are excited to show you not only what is going on in your buyers' brains but what you can do about it. *Hold on!*

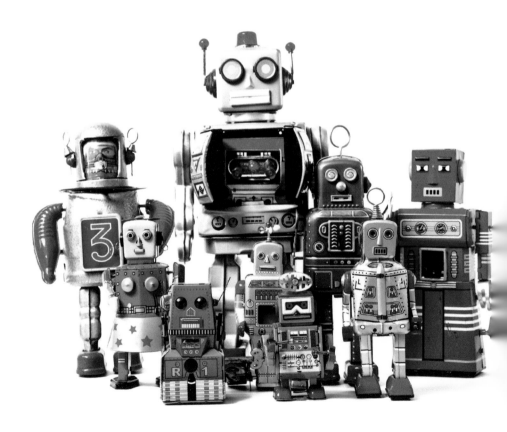

Key Takeaways

- Content marketing offers a way to educate your prospects and generate preference for your firm.

- There are specific tactics used by firms that consistently win in competitive situations.

- Your professional services brand is the product of your reputation and your visibility.

- Research is key to understanding your clients.

- Specialization and positioning help companies choose your firm over less differentiated competitors.

- Firms that focus on brand building have a strong advantage in the marketplace.

CASE STUDY

At Syska Hennessy, Buying Is About Relationships

SYSKA HENNESSY
GROUP

As Director of Communications at Syska Hennessy Group, a global leader in engineering, design and commissioning, Mary Moore is in charge of all internal and external communications, including Syska's corporate website, blog, newsletters, publications and other communications. When selecting a service provider, she has three criteria:

Reputation: Mary feels more confident hiring a "prominent brand in the industry." So how do you increase your reputation with her? "Provide value to the marketplace before you even make the sale," Mary advises. "If you're a contributor to your community, then you're visible." Mary keeps abreast of industry trends, looking out for online thought leaders. "When someone shares a new whitepaper, thought, article, idea or image. with me, I really like that," Mary says. "If you put a good product out there," she says, "your clients will come to you."

Trust: When Mary is hiring a service provider, she says that it's important to have some familiarity and trust already built up. That feeling of trust is often created prior to the sale, by a "person knowing me enough to keep their eyes open, to send me information that is helpful." When a seller takes the time to send her relevant, helpful information that makes her job easier, Mary will think of the seller when she requires a relevant service or product.

Follow through: Mary's "go-to" service providers — the ones that she turns to time and again — are the firms that continue "to make her look good" over time. The best providers help make her job easier by anticipating needs, staying abreast of industry trends, sending valuable information and over-delivering on promises.

According to Mary, the biggest mistake service providers make is "incorrect targeting through communications." Mary receives about a dozen cold calls a day from sellers touting services and products, many of whom are confused about her role and Syska's mission. Often, she says, "it's obvious that these people haven't done their research, as the products have nothing to do with what I do." These phone calls are time-wasters for Mary, and they leave her less likely to hire the firms that have contacted her in this way.

"Don't just go out there and sell," says Mary. "Be a thought leader! Be a presence! Whatever your sector is, go out and contribute!"

CHAPTER 3
The Research

The inspiration for this book was a body of research we conducted on professional services firms over a period of years. We were eager to understand what motivated buyers of services so that we could help firms that sell services become better marketers.

Three Studies

In 2009, we published our original buyers study in which we interviewed 137 buyers of professional services. Then four years later we conducted an entirely new study. Using a mix of phone interviews and surveys, we researched 822 buyers and 533 sellers of professional services. Buyers and sellers were matched. The buyers bought services from the sellers. This allowed us to study both sides of the relationship.

Figure 3.1. Research Sample Composition

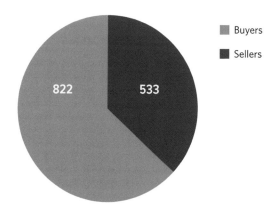

■ Buyers

■ Sellers

We wanted to answer key questions, such as:

- How do buyers choose one firm over another?

- What characteristics are buyers looking for in a firm?

- How should firms be marketing their services?

- How do companies that need services determine which firms to include in their search?

- What factors contribute to strong client loyalty?

For the first time, we have a strong understanding of what is going on inside the buyer's brain.

We did our latest research in conjunction with a separate study of buyers conducted by the Boston-based consultancy RAIN Group. Their study of over 700 B2B sales opportunities represented $3.1 billion in annual purchases. The study focused on the sales process and revealed critical insights into the way firms that win competitive bids differ from those that come in second place. We cover this data and its implications on professional services sales in Chapter 6.

How We Segmented the Data

In addition to studying the aggregate data, we also looked at the findings from other angles. We examined, for instance, the responses from five major professional services groups:

- Accounting and Finance

- Architecture, Engineering and Construction

- Management Consulting

- Technology Services

- Law Firms and Legal Services

In many situations, we found that the different industries had significantly different results. We'll point out the important differences along the way.

Figure 3.2. Overall Composition of Study by Industry

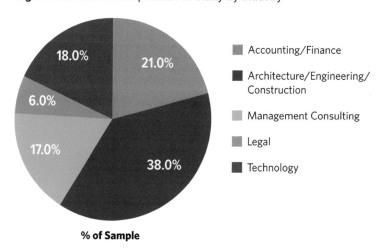

% of Sample

Of course, where applicable, we segment the data by buyer and seller, which (as we described in Chapter 1) reveals significant differences in the way the two groups approach certain issues. It is this perspective that informs the bulk of this book and helps us peer into the brains of prospective buyers.

In many situations, we found that the different industries offer significantly different results.

For the first time, with data from more than 2,000 buyers and sellers, we feel like we have solid answers to these questions — and a strong understanding of what is going on inside the buyer's brain.

In Part II of this book we'll dig more deeply into this data and tease out its significance for sellers like you.

Key Takeaways

- This book is based on a significant body of data from three separate studies of buyers and sellers of professional services.

- The most recent study was designed to look at both sides of the relationship.

- We interviewed or surveyed almost 1,500 individuals.

- We supplemented our sample with data from over 700 sales opportunities.

- We segmented the data by industry and buyers versus sellers.

- We sought to answer critical questions about the motivations, perceptions and preferences of buyers of professional services.

PART II:
Lessons Learned

Find the gap, then close it.

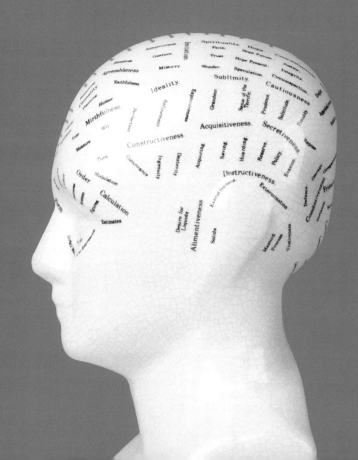

CHAPTER 4
Target the Right Clients

N ot all clients are created equal. Your firm will be a poor match for some clients. While they see your services as necessary, some clients don't consider your firm essential to their success. They may even view your firm as an expense to be minimized — one that could, if necessary, easily be replaced.

At the same time, you may have a very different relationship with other clients. Your services are essential to solving their key problems. They consider your firm a highly valued and trusted team member that would be difficult, if not impossible, to replace. And the value you add makes your fees seem more than fair. Your competitive advantage is nearly insurmountable.

What is different in these scenarios is not your firm. It's the client. In one scenario you are a disposable commodity. In the other you are a value creator. Who wouldn't like to have more clients in the latter category and fewer in the former?

To get there you need to understand your potential clients and what's holding them back. What are their most important challenges? These are likely to be your best opportunities to add significant value.

Buyers' Business Challenges

We asked both buyers and sellers to identify the most significant business challenges faced by buyers' organization. Figure 4.1 shows their top 10 responses.

Figure 4.1. Top 10 Business Challenges as Seen by Buyers and Sellers

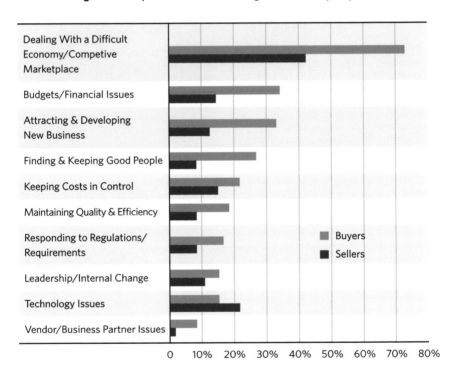

When you look at this figure, a couple of things are immediately obvious. First, companies deal with a wide range of issues. And while it's not apparent from this chart, there can be important industry differences, as well.[1]

---

1 For more on these differences, see the Resources section of this book for links to our industry-specific *How Buyers Buy* reports.

Second, across this wide range of issues a pattern emerges. There is a gap between buyers and sellers. Sellers misunderstand buyers' challenges.

This is a critical divide. If sellers do not understand the extent and nature of their clients' business challenges it will be hard for them to bring significant value to the relationship.

Sellers underestimate buyers' challenges.

But the situation gets worse. There is another a gap. And this one opens up like a chasm between the sellers' services and the clients' problems.

Relevance of the Seller's Services

How important are the sellers' services in addressing the challenges that buyers struggle with? As it turns out there are some important industry differences.

We asked buyers and sellers in each of our study's four industry groups to rate the importance of the seller's services to solving the buyer's challenges. Figure 4.2 shows the proportion of buyers and sellers giving the seller's services top importance ratings (ratings of 9 or 10 on a 0-10 scale).

Figure 4.2. Proportion of Buyers and Sellers Giving Sellers' Services Top Ratings for Their Importance to Solving Key Business Challenges

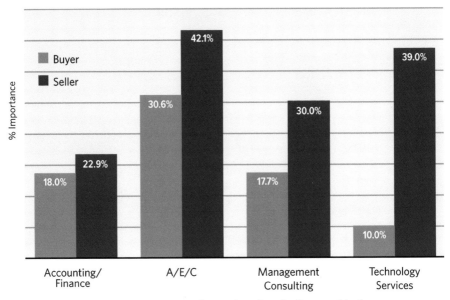

How important are the services that the firm provides?

There are some industry differences worth noting. The architecture, engineering and construction group is seen as being comparatively more relevant to its clients' key issues than, for instance, technology, which is the least relevant. If you think about it, this makes sense. Without architects and engineers, buildings can't get designed or built. Technology, however, is less often at the center of an organization's agenda.

> The sharper your focus, the more likely you are to understanding your clients' challenges.

The most important insights from this set of data, however, are the differences between buyers' and sellers' ratings of relevance. Sellers consistently overestimate the importance of their services. In the case of technology services this difference is quite sizable. In accounting and financial services, it is more modest.

Closing the Relevance Gap

Clearly, buyers and sellers see the key issues differently. And they disagree about how relevant or important sellers' services are to addressing them. This gap can be closed in three different ways.

First, do a better job of targeting clients. Focus your firm's attention on marketing to clients whose needs you understand. The most common way to do this is to specialize in certain types of organizations. The sharper your focus, the more likely you are to understand your clients' challenges.

Second, conduct systematic research on your target client groups. This will allow you to offer more relevant services based on a better understanding of client needs and perceptions. In fact, a previous study demonstrated that firms that conduct systematic research tend to grow faster and are more profitable. We explored these findings in depth in our book *Spiraling Up.*[2] As you may remember from Chapter 1, firms that conducted frequent research on target clients outperformed those that conducted occasional or no research, with those that did frequent research showing significantly higher growth and profitability.

2 For a link to *Spiraling Up*, see the Resources section at the back of this book.

And third, do a better job of communicating how your services address key organizational challenges. This approach is most helpful when your service has a greater impact than your client appreciates. We'll talk more about this later.

In most cases, your firm will see the greatest positive impact when you embrace all three of these approaches. We'll discuss how to accomplish this in Part III of this book.

Meet the Competition

Most of us in the professional services feel like we have a pretty good handle on our competition. We often know which companies have beat us in competitive bid situations, and we have a general sense of which firms lead the industry. The only problem is, we are usually wrong.

How can that be? Consider this. If you were to ask your staff to list your competitors then ask your clients to do the same, you would produce two lists that have surprisingly little in common. Typically, there is only a 25% overlap in the lists of competitors produced by a seller and its buyers.

Figure 4.3. Buyers and Sellers Competitor Lists Show Minimal Overlap

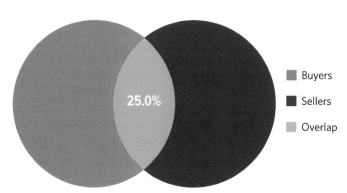

25.0%

■ Buyers

■ Sellers

■ Overlap

In our experience, this disparity has two root causes. First, sellers tend to make fine distinctions between firms and their capabilities. As a result, they rule out many potential competitors based on their insider understanding of the industry (a seller might think, for example, "There is no way Firm Y could do that."). Potential clients, on the other hand, make no such judgments because they lack the technical knowledge to evaluate firms in this way.

> There is only a 25% overlap in the lists of competitors produced by a seller and its buyers.

The second root cause is that clients tend to entertain a range of competitors depending on how they diagnose or think about a challenge. For example, a business may be experiencing declining revenue. Depending on how the company thinks about that issue it could seek out a sales trainer to increase revenue, a cost cutting consultant to improve the bottom line or a new product guru to help launch a new product. A single problem can have many different cures. And different narratives around the nature of a challenge can produce very different competitors.

The bottom line? The way you define the problem to your client can have far reaching consequences. We'll explore this issue further in the next chapter.

Key Takeaways

- Sellers misunderstand the extent and nature of client challenges.

- Sellers also overestimate the perceived importance of their service in solving key challenges.

- This gap can be closed by better targeting, systematic research or better communication of your services' impact.

- A seller's list of competitors has little overlap with the buyer's list.

- Owning the narrative around problem definition has important competitive implications.

CASE STUDY

Selling to Big Fed: How to Win, and Keep, a Government Service Contract

Hinge conducted a private interview with a buyer who handles procurement for a major government agency. In order to provide candid insights and to protect his agency against possible conflicts of interest, the buyer has elected to remain anonymous and will be referred to by his first name, "John." At his agency, John controls a $20 million annual budget for capital projects including facility and infrastructure improvements that require A/E design services: architecture, landscape, preservation, structural, mechanical, electrical, plumbing and environmental engineering.

Understanding IDIQ
If you want a piece of John's $20 million budget, you'll have to apply for an IDIQ contract with his agency. IDIQ is an acronym for "indefinite delivery, indefinite quantity," a type of open-

ended contract that gives an agency permission to buy as many services as needed from a vendor during a fixed period of time—usually about 10 years. Winning an IDIQ contract is key, as John is required to hire from his agency's small pool of 13 to 15 IDIQ vendors whenever there is a new project.

Every few years, there are opportunities for new contractors to win admission into this IDIQ pool. When this happens, John has to follow certain strict protocols to ensure that selection is fair and transparent. The solicitation request is detailed and includes a long list of criteria. Governed by Federal Acquisition Regulations (FAR) and the Brooks Act, his agency must publicize the request for proposals (RFPs) openly, typically listing the solicitation within the FedBizOps website.

Culling the herd

John usually receives upwards of 75 proposals for such a solicitation. Once the RFP timeframe has closed, all of the application packages are screened against the criteria listed in the RFP such as "past performance, technical abilities, resumes of key personnel, financial viability, related project experience and current or projected workload — to prove you have the capacity to handle the needs of our agency."

According to John, culling the large pool of applicants is fairly easy, as many firms make obvious blunders in their proposals that prevent them from qualifying. "You would be surprised," he says. "Many of them don't provide answers to how they will handle the myriad services that we require. Will you use subcontractors or consultants? Can you do the work yourself? If someone fails to address all of the criteria in our RFP, they're an easy out."

CASE STUDY

Quality, not cost

Contrary to popular belief, vendors' rates are not considered in the selection process. The purpose of the A/E solicitation is to get the most qualified of all interested vendors. The selection criteria within a RFP typically place a premium on relevant experience as demonstrated by performance, technical abilities and personnel qualifications.

"We are looking for people who go above and beyond," John says. Being an experienced industry leader can be helpful at this point in selection, and it's good to highlight recognized work and awards; but John and his panel aren't always looking for "star-chitects." "If we need someone to build a sewer," John says, "we don't really care if you're an industry star known for designing museums, libraries or public spaces."

Once the applicant pool has been culled to about 10 top-quality firms, John and his panel will call vendor references to have frank conversations. "Do they perform? What is their quality of work? What it's like to work with them?" Each of the top 10 is then ranked for the selection criteria listed in the RFP and assigned a numerical grade. Depending on how close these numerical grades are, and how many new IDIQ slots are available, 3 to 6 top firms will be offered the opportunity to interview.

Nailing the interview

According to John, the interviews are a great way to see how knowledgeable a firm really is. "Nobody knows what questions will be asked ahead of time, because the questions are based on their presentations. We want to see how you will handle yourself. Can you answer our questions with depth? If you get flustered, that looks bad."

The interview is also an important time to assess the personalities and cultures of firms and managers. "You'll be working with these guys day in and day out for 10 years," John says. "Let's face it: we don't want to deal with difficult personalities."

IDIQ is not a guarantee of work
The firms that make it through this rigorous process (sometimes just one firm, sometimes as many as three) are awarded an IDIQ contract for the next 10 years. But winning an IDIQ isn't an instant guarantee of a decade of work. Although John's agency tries to balance the workload among eligible firms, vendors that don't produce quality work may find themselves on the outside, "blackballed by certain facilities."

And even with 13 to 15 firms in the IDIQ pool, John turns to his handful of "go-to" firms first. John's go-to firms are the ones that have proven to him that they can provide quality again and again; some of them even have design studios dedicated exclusively to his agency.

When the IDIQ contract comes to an end, there's no guarantee that a firm will be reselected. John says, "They have to submit a package like everyone else. We've had some excellent firms who did not get picked back up. They didn't put the effort in for the new proposal."

The moral of the story? "Don't get lazy," John advises. "Every time you do a project for us, you should treat it like it's the first time."

CHAPTER 5
Make the Connection

Your next clients are looking for you. They just don't know where to find you. They've asked their friends and colleagues. They've searched online. Some are looking right at you — and they still can't see you. They can't tell who you are, what you do and how you can help them.

Now that you've closed the relevance gap — you've identified your best target clients and figured out how to relate your services to their key challenges — it's time to let the world of potential clients know you're out there.

Right now, as far as your prospective clients are concerned, you are invisible. You've been hiding in plain sight. By understanding what clients are looking for — and where they're looking for it — you can put your firm in a more strategic position with potential buyers. You'll help them find you.

Looking for Help
We've already determined that potential clients are trying to find you — or your competitors. How can you make sure that your firm is the one that pops up on their radar screens? A good place to start is by figuring out where exactly the client is looking.

We wanted to understand how buyers go about searching for the help they need. Where do they look when they want to find a new firm? In our research, we heard the same response again and again: More than 70% of buyers ask a friend or colleague for a recommendation. Naturally, a colleague will recommend a firm with a good track record. In other words, your good reputation and high visibility are key.

Figure 5.1. How Buyers Search for a New Professional Services Firm

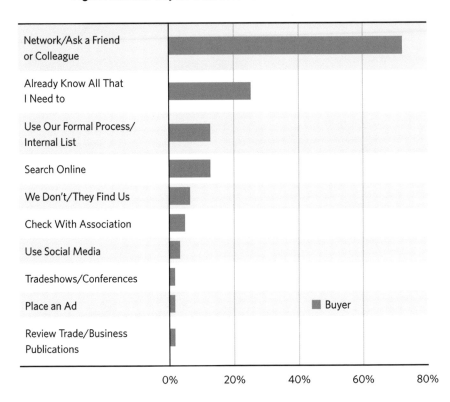

From the perspective of some buyers, there is no need to look at all. Almost 1 in 4 buyers say they already knew enough about the market to find a suitable seller. Another 11% are forced to follow their company's formal procurement process.

Outside of those responses, the next most frequent avenue for finding sellers, at 11%, was an online search. It's a sign of the times that Internet inquiries easily outpace more traditional approaches like consulting with a professional association (3%), attending trade shows (1%) or responding to an ad (1%). Clearly, your reputation follows you online.

In a separate line of questioning, we asked buyers for the best way to market to them. Their top answer — given by 47% or respondents — was to develop a reputation for producing results.

> 70% of buyers ask a friend or colleague for a recommendation.

All of the responses underscored the importance of developing a widely recognized reputation — and they made a compelling case for developing a strong brand. As we described in Chapter 2, your brand is your reputation combined with your visibility. Prospective buyers turn to people they trust — their friends and colleagues — for recommendations. The stronger your reputation and the better your visibility the greater the likelihood that they will recommend your firm. (So pay attention to your brand. In Part III of this book, we'll show you how.)

How Online Search Can Drive Referrals

Let's set aside for a moment the folks who ask for referrals and the people who already have a vendor (or vendors) in mind. We already know that building your brand is going to be the best way to reach them.

That leaves online search — the second most popular way buyers find potential service providers. Many more clients search for sellers online than through traditional marketing channels. And we believe this method will only become more popular over time. But are Internet searches really a game-changer? Can they influence those all-important colleagues whom the buyer turns to for recommendations?

At our own firm, we learned firsthand just how important a strong online presence can be. We were once contacted by the managing partner of a regional accounting firm. When we asked him how he learned about us, he explained that one of his colleagues downloaded a copy of our book *Spiraling Up* from our website. He found it online while searching for advice on growing their firm.

So, on one level, our newest client was referred to us by a colleague. On another level, that referral was the direct result of an online search. Both colleague referrals and a strong online presence — not to mention traditional marketing tools — are important in generating new business opportunities. Don't rely on just one or the other. You need all of the above!

Measuring Brand Strength

How can you tell if your brand is powerful enough to attract new clients? Is there a way to measure the overall strength of your brand?

| Many more clients search for sellers online than through traditional marketing channels.

It stands to reason that if we could find a formula for gauging your firm's reputation and its visibility, we would also be able to determine the strength of your brand.

Now, it's important to point out that you should only measure your brand strength among your target client group, not the general public. After all, every one of your new clients and referrals will come from this group. And chances are, you will not be actively promoting your brand to the general public, so your awareness there will be much lower.

You may also want to take stock of perceptions within your firm. It's a good idea to measure your brand strength as viewed by your firm's leadership and staff. This way, you can compare the results to outside perceptions and determine how accurately your team understands its position in the marketplace.

Figure 5.2 shows the proportion of buyers and sellers who rated the seller's reputation as "very good" (a rating of 9 or 10). Note that it was the buyers who had a more favorable view of the sellers' reputation: 57% of buyers and only 34% sellers gave it a high rating.

Figure 5.2. Percentage of Buyers and Sellers Rating Seller's Reputation as 9 or 10 (Using a 1-10 scale, where 10 is the highest)

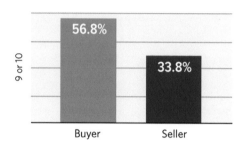

This same pattern holds for marketplace visibility ratings. In Figure 5.3, we see that sellers again rated their own visibility lower than buyers (23% vs. 8%).

Figure 5.3. Percentage of Buyers and Sellers Rating Seller's Visibility as 9 or 10 (Using a 1-10 scale, where 10 is the highest)

Why do sellers rate their reputation and marketplace visibility lower than do their clients? While our research didn't specifically address this question, we can offer a couple of possible explanations. For one thing, all professionals are insiders: they see and struggle with the flaws in their business every day, but these problems may be invisible or inconsequential to clients. In addition, sellers are on the wrong side of the fence to evaluate their standing in the marketplace. Because they're not buyers, seeking out and evaluating the options, they simply don't have the perspective to compare themselves to their competitors.

Sellers don't always sell themselves short — think back to Chapter 4, where you may recall that sellers rated their own relevance to buyers' key challenges higher than did buyers themselves. Sometimes the misperception runs in the other direction.

The Visibility Gap

Notice that the marketplace visibility ratings in these graphs are much lower than the reputation rankings. Among buyers, professional services firms tend to have good reputations, with 57% of buyers rating them as "very good." But just a paltry 23% of buyers thought the sellers' visibility was "very good." Most sellers have a marketplace awareness problem. We refer to this as the Visibility Gap.

Figure 5.4. Buyers Ratings of Seller's Reputation and Visibility (Using a 1-10 scale, where 10 is the highest)

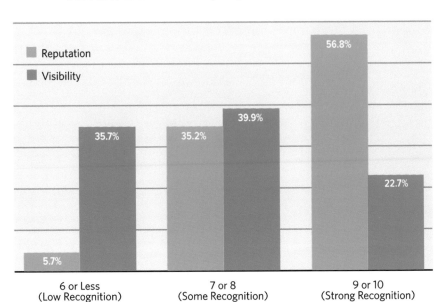

6 or Less (Low Recognition)
7 or 8 (Some Recognition)
9 or 10 (Strong Recognition)

Many firms work overtime to offer high quality services to their clients. The reward? Loyal clients who love your work. You develop a great reputation among your devoted stable of clients.

In other words, you're loved by the clients who know you well.

But that is where your brand falters.

A great reputation does not on its own translate into high marketplace visibility. Instead, your firm must narrow the gap between your reputation and your marketplace visibility. If not, your brand will languish.

Closing the Gap

So how do you do you close the visibility gap? Is it as simple as spending more money on display ads? Unfortunately, it's not that easy. If it were, many more firms would be well known in the marketplace.

You need to do more than tell the world that your firm exists. To strengthen your brand, you must convey your strong reputation as you increase your visibility. The two must work together.

> A great reputation does not, on its own, translate into high marketplace visibility.

One of the most effective ways to build your reputation and increase your visibility is to embrace content marketing. Content marketing works like this: your firm develops a wide variety of educational content targeted at different stages of the buying cycle. Examples of these pieces include blog posts, guides, white papers, videos, webinars, articles, e-books, newsletters and research reports (to name just a few). You give away most, if not all, of these pieces of content for free. But in the case of the longer pieces with more perceived value you require that individuals exchange a small amount of personal information (such as their name and email address) for the document. This allows you to build an email list to which you can promote more relevant content. The strategy has a number of advantages:

1. It attracts highly qualified leads.
2. It keeps people engaged because they want or need to become educated.
3. It positions you as an expert: you are the teacher; they are the pupils.
4. When people realize they don't have the time or resources to fix the problem themselves, your firm will be the first they call.
5. Because your content sits on your website, it can reach people in new markets across the country or the world.

Today, content marketing is rapidly gaining traction in the professional services community[1]. But does this educational approach to marketing actually work in the real world? Does it translate into new business?

---

1 To learn more about content marketing and how it fits into a broader online marketing program, download our free book, *Online Marketing for Professional Services*:
http://www.hingemarketing.com/library/article/online_marketing_for_professional_services

Win the Narrative, Win the Sale

There's a telling clue in the RAIN Group data on over 700 complex sales. It identified the qualities that separated the winners from the also-rans.

A total of 42 different factors were examined to pinpoint what the successful sellers did right — and the runners-up didn't. One of those factors caught our attention. And get this: it was rated number 1 for the winners and dead last for the runners-up.

That factor was "educate me with new ideas or perspectives." The winners did it. The losers did not.

It makes perfect sense. Educating potential clients and giving them new perspectives conveys your good reputation and, at the same time, bolsters your visibility. It also addresses the relevance gap we described in Chapter 4.

> "Educate me with new ideas or perspectives." The winners did it. The losers did not.

Think about it: You help potential clients see their situation in a new light. You guide them through alternative solutions. You directly influence the way they think about their problem. And as they work with you, your new clients begin to trust and even rely on your expertise. It soon becomes clear that your solution makes sense — and that your firm is the right choice for the job.

You aren't just finding people who have an immediate need for your services. You are connecting with prospective clients who have a challenge that your firm can solve. And you are helping them understand that challenge in a way that highlights the relevance of your services.

Congratulations! You have the buyer's attention. The next hurdle is closing the sale.

Key Takeaways

- When searching for a new provider, 70% of buyers turn first to a friend or colleague for recommendations.

- To generate more of these referrals in the marketplace, you need a good reputation and high visibility. In other words, you need a strong brand.

- A combination of online and traditional marketing is the ideal way to accomplish this task.

- Most firms need to increase marketplace visibility while maintaining their reputation.

- Educating your potential clients is a great way to build your brand while influencing the way they define their problem.

CASE STUDY

The Ideal Seller

powering your transformation journey

What does the perfect vendor look like? Eric Hansen is a managing partner at organizational and leadership consulting firm Navalent, and he shared what his team searches for when hiring outside accounting and financial services.

Value match: Navalent is clear about its company values; any sign of shady business or sour past relationships is a deal breaker. They need a provider they can trust.

Competence and reputation: Has the seller solved similar problems in the past? If so, are their clients satisfied? Having a sound reputation and proof of competence is a must.

Understanding: If a seller takes the time to fully understand a buyer's problems, they have a good chance of winning the job. According to Eric, "Being able to understand our challenges and propose the right solution is more important than having an existing personal relationship."

Local (if possible): Navalent is a small company, so the firm likes to support other small and medium-sized businesses. If a contractor works within the same community, that's even better. Working with smaller vendors often leads to more intimate relationships.

Thought leadership: "Intellectual capital and an online presence really do matter," explains Eric. "I look for publications or some expression of intellectual depth when evaluating a company online."

For sellers, getting in the door is just the start. The next step is to transform that contract into an ongoing partnership. Following are the keys to a long-term relationship in the eyes of Eric and his team:

Ease of business: Contractors that focus on making the buyer's life easier will increase their chances of a long-term relationship. If there are processes in place to support smooth transactions and the billing process is seamless, the buyer will be happy.

Flexibility: Firms that are willing to work extra hours, take on custom projects, and cater services to fit the unique needs of a buyer are more likely to stick around.

Proactivity: Buyers look for a company that sees challenges ahead of time and recommends proactive solutions.

Communicate with simplicity: Service providers should avoid jargon that non-specialists don't understand. Buyers appreciate partners who can explain complex issues clearly — and make them look good in front of their clients.

Royal treatment: "If you don't treat me as an important client," says Eric, "then I won't consider you a reliable partner." With larger sellers, showing an equal level of appreciation and attention to all clients — big or small — can be a key to future business.

CHAPTER
Closing the Sale

6

O ne of your potential clients has a problem. She's already spent a lot of time and resources looking for a solution. And the only thing she's discovered is that she can't do this on her own. She needs outside help. That's where you come in.

This prospect has come to the realization that she needs a professional services provider — and, luckily, you're on her short list. Perhaps your brand was strong enough to generate a referral. Or maybe your SEO (search engine optimization) was powerful enough to attract her attention. Either way, she has selected your firm as a possible candidate to solve her problem.

Now it's time to turn that prospect into a client. It's time to close the sale.

Careful Criteria
Where to begin? The sales-closing process typically starts with the buyers developing a clear sense of what they want in a service provider. Think of this as formulating the selection criteria.

The criteria can vary from buyer to buyer. Some are fairly informal and loose. Others follow a highly structured process. In the case of, say, government procurement, the criteria may be specified in an RFP. There may even be a formal weighting system for each criterion.

Figure 6.1 identifies the most important buyer selection criteria. Having a good reputation tops the list.

Figure 6.1. Top Selection Criteria

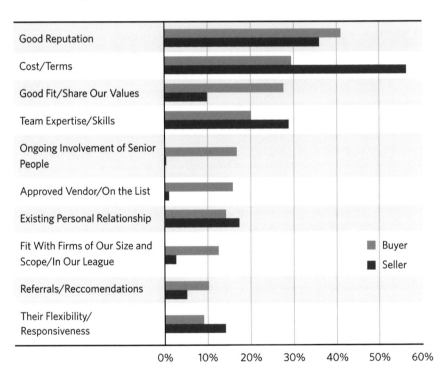

Interestingly, sellers have a relatively accurate view of their reputation's importance. They don't over or under value it. That's not the case, however, when it comes to the issue of pricing. Sellers vastly overestimate the importance of cost to their buyers. The margin isn't even close. More than 50% of sellers say price is among the key drivers in a buyer's decision. But only 28% of buyers rate price that highly.

We see a similar story when we look at the importance of cultural fit or shared values between buyers and sellers. But this time, the views are reversed. Buyers rate this cultural symmetry at the same level of importance as price. But this time, it's sellers who underestimate its significance — by a wide margin.

Buyers and sellers differ on several other factors, as well. Sellers underestimate the importance of ongoing involvement from their senior staff. Sellers also give little consideration to the size of their firm. Buyers want a firm that has experience "playing in their league."

> Sellers vastly overestimate the importance of cost to their buyers. The margin isn't even close.

Look at it from the buyer's perspective: At this point in the selection process, buyers are looking for a firm that is capable of engaging them at the appropriate professional level. They want a firm that has a strong reputation for solving their specific challenges. Price, while not insignificant, does not loom as large for them as it does for the seller.

The right selection criteria will help a buyer choose your firm. These criteria can, in effect, rule you in. But there are other criteria that can just as quickly rule you out.

Landmines: How to Avoid Blowing Up Your Buyers
What kind of circumstances might persuade a buyer to rule out your firm?

Often, poor past experiences with other firms leave a bad taste in buyers' mouths. You can practically hear the pain in some buyers' voices: "That last firm promised us the moon. I should have known they couldn't deliver." "Why can't we find a firm that isn't like all the others?" "Is the right fit really out there?"

Figure 6.2 details the most common landmines buyers try to sidestep in the selection process. Topping the not-to-do list are 1) breaking your promises and 2) being indistinguishable from other firms. Sellers underestimate the importance of both factors.

Figure 6.2. What Buyers Want to Avoid

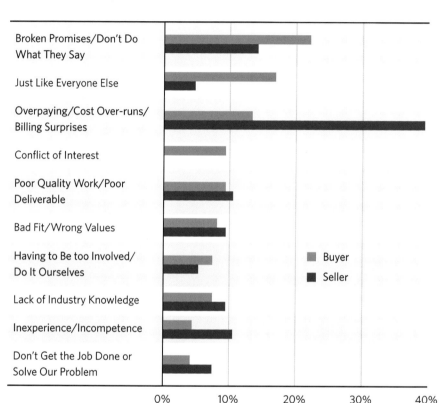

Sellers once again put too much emphasis on the cost or billing dimension of their relationships. Even as they worry about how much to charge, they fail to realize that they are undervaluing what clients want most — sellers who keep their word and prove that they are different from the run-of-the-mill firm. By misinterpreting the factors that are most important to your client, you may find yourself ruled out, and not even realize why.

Tipping the Scales
It's time for the final selection. So far, your firm has done everything right. You have paid attention to the correct selection criteria. You've noted those factors that might rule you out to

clients. But in the final selection process, what will ultimately tip the scale in your favor? How will you end up the winner?

Figure 6.3. What Tips the Scale for the Winner?

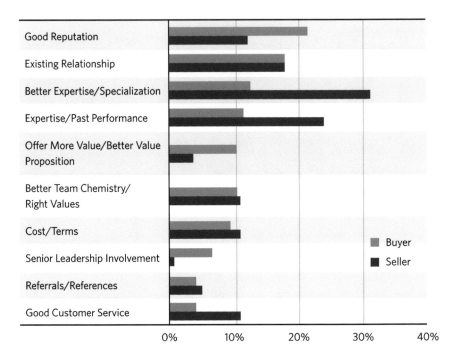

Sellers generally believe that when push comes to shove the top factors in their favor are expertise and experience. But they dramatically overestimate the significance of those items to the client.

While both buyers and sellers see the importance of existing relationships accurately, sellers underestimate the role that their reputation plays in the final selection. Also, a strong reputation is the one factor that can overcome an existing relationship. Put another way, having a strong reputation is the easiest way to unseat an incumbent.

Buyers want to know that you can deliver on your promises to solve their problem. So how do you convince them that your firm is a good choice? Fortunately, the research suggests an answer.

> Having a strong reputation is the easiest way to unseat an incumbent.

Winners Sell Differently

Closing the sale is not just about having the right factors in place. It's also about effectively communicating those factors as you engage your potential clients.

With the help of our friends at RAIN Group, we examined 42 separate factors to determine how the firms that won the sale distinguished themselves from those that came in second. If there's one thing we learned from this cooperative research study, it's that winners sell very differently than runners-up.

Ten factors combined to predict success in closing the sale. Most intriguingly, these factors also forecasted the clients' satisfaction with the purchasing process and their intention to purchase additional services from the same firm. These factors are shown in Figure 6.4. You can think of them as a checklist of the steps

you must take to successfully close the professional services sale.

Figure 6.4. What Sales Winners Do Differently[1]

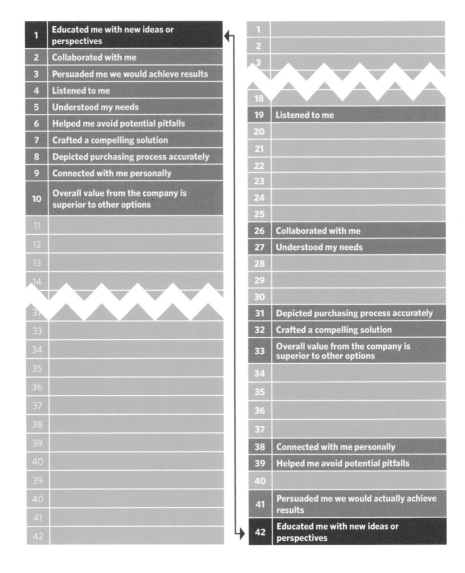

1	Educated me with new ideas or perspectives
2	Collaborated with me
3	Persuaded me we would achieve results
4	Listened to me
5	Understood my needs
6	Helped me avoid potential pitfalls
7	Crafted a compelling solution
8	Depicted purchasing process accurately
9	Connected with me personally
10	Overall value from the company is superior to other options
11	
12	
13	
14	
37	
33	
34	
35	
36	
37	
38	
39	
40	
39	
40	
41	
42	

1	
2	
3	
18	
19	Listened to me
20	
21	
22	
23	
24	
25	
26	Collaborated with me
27	Understood my needs
28	
29	
30	
31	Depicted purchasing process accurately
32	Crafted a compelling solution
33	Overall value from the company is superior to other options
34	
35	
36	
37	
38	Connected with me personally
39	Helped me avoid potential pitfalls
40	
41	Persuaded me we would actually achieve results
42	Educated me with new ideas or perspectives

---

1 "What Sales Winners Do Differently" by Mike Schultz and John Doerr, RAIN Group.

You'll notice that, in some cases, winners do a better job of taking care of the basics, like listening to and understanding prospects' needs, crafting compelling solutions and connecting on a personal level. Botch these and you can forget about your chances of winning the client.

> Educating your prospective client turns out to be a great strategy for a variety of reasons.

But the professional services sales process is complex. And simply covering the basics is no longer enough. Let's take a closer look at the top three factors that separate winners from second-place finishers.

Factor 1: Educate me with new ideas or perspectives

This should look familiar to you. We touched on it in Chapter 5. Educating your prospective client turns out to be a great strategy for a variety of reasons. It boosts your reputation and raises your firm's visibility at the same time. How do you educate your potential clients? With blog posts, webinars, articles, whitepapers, e-books and free consultations. These are the tools of a content marketing strategy.

> It's not enough to expect potential clients to accept your solutions at face value.

When prospects become your students, an interesting thing happens: you quickly become an authority in your area of expertise and a trusted resource. In short, your brand grows stronger. As a result, these prospect-students are very likely to refer you in an appropriate situation.

You also give potential clients a window into your expertise and thought process. In effect, you are offering them a sample of the way your firm works.

And, perhaps most importantly, you are able to shape the conversation around your prospective clients' challenges. You help them diagnose their problem and craft the solution. It is a great start to a winning strategy.

Factor 2: Collaborate with me

Buyers want solutions that address their specific challenges. This is where collaboration really pays off.

When you work hand in hand with your prospective clients, you have the opportunity to demonstrate how you shape the solution that best solves their problem.

Instead of imposing your own rigid solution — being a "my way or the highway" seller — you work with clients to help them solve their problems in a way that highlights your strengths and theirs. It's a win-win arrangement.

Factor 3: Persuade me that we will achieve results

I'm your prospective client. Thanks to you, I now understand the true dimensions of my problem. You have helped me see it in a fresh and creative light. And you've collaborated with me to devise a reasonable solution.

There's just one more wrinkle. How can I be sure that your solution will produce the promised results?

It's not enough to expect potential clients to accept your solutions at face value. You must convince them that your plan will perform as promised. The proof could take any number of forms, from case studies to client references to formal research. Whatever form it takes, it must be persuasive — or you risk losing the sale. If possible, your proof should demonstrate that you have solved similar problems before for similar clients. If you can't meet this standard, draw on the best evidence you have. It can dramatically improve your win rate.

An Architect's Story

Kevin, a partner in a boutique residential architecture firm, was looking for new ways to grow his firm. In a tough economy, his once-plentiful referrals were drying up. So instead of waiting for clients to come to him, he decided to go out and engage clients himself.

He had heard about architects who were blogging and interacting with prospects online to answer questions about home design and renovation. It seemed like a natural way to get involved with people who wanted what he had to offer.

Educating with content marketing
So Kevin invested in a blog for his website. He arranged his schedule so he could produce a post each week. He decided to write on topics that answered common questions he had encountered in his practice — issues such as energy efficiency, how much to budget for a new home design, the pros and cons of different construction materials, and why architects are worth the extra investment. With the help of a marketing firm, he incorporated important keyword phrases into his writing so that people searching the Internet would be able to find his content online.

A social approach to collaboration
He also began participating in a number of Google+ groups where people interested in home architecture gather to discuss issues and ask questions. Rather than passively monitor the conversations, he jumped in and became an active participant, answering a wide range of questions and suggesting better ways people might accomplish their goals.

The payoff
It wasn't long before Kevin received his first email from a woman who wanted him to bid on an extension for her house. Soon, similar emails and calls began coming in on a weekly basis.

Encouraged by this response, he began writing beefier pieces — educational guides — and posting them on his website. Later Kevin turned these into a full-length e-book, which he gave away in exchange for a people's email addresses. The demand for this book astonished him. Apparently the word was getting out.

Then one day a gentleman from across the country called. He told Kevin he was ready to hire his firm. No bidding. No competitors. The man said he loved the houses they designed and he was impressed by Kevin's appreciation of a home's finer details. When and how could they get started?

Wow. That had never happened before!

A little persuasion goes a long way
Of course, not all sales were that easy. Kevin learned that it sometimes took a little persuasion to give his prospects the confidence to buy from him. He had to convince them that after spending all that money they weren't going to be disappointed. Fortunately, Kevin already had a lot of delighted clients. So the first thing he did was give each prospect a long list of references. "Choose any of them. Or call them all," he would tell them. "You'll get an interesting perspective from each one." He also shared case studies of some of his favorite projects, presenting them in their very best light with beautiful photography and compelling testimonials. And of course, he pointed prospective clients to his growing library of educational materials so that they could learn more about the design process — and his firm's mastery of it.

Whenever people showed more than passing interest in his architecture firm, Kevin would offer to discuss their project with them. He would be happy to give them advice and help them think through the details of their new home. Once people realized that he wasn't asking for anything in return, they came to trust him and his opinions.

Not surprisingly, the majority of these folks hired Kevin's firm. And why shouldn't they? He gave them an immersive experience: educating them, persuading them and collaborating with them.

A Model for Success

Now that we've explored the research behind closing the sale, how do those lessons stack up with our earlier insights into the perceptions and expectations of potential clients? In fact, we find that a model to acquire new clients is starting to take shape.

> By solving client issues and delivering enhanced value, your reputation for producing results grows.

We've learned the importance of having a clear target client. You must understand enough about the client's business to identify the areas where you can add the greatest value. Put another way, you must be able to close all the perception gaps that are so common among professional services firms. Think of this as developing a strategic brand.

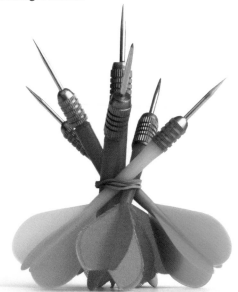

Building on this heightened level of understanding, you're in a position to educate your potential clients and help them develop new insights. The solutions you offer should come out of that understanding. And content marketing is an ideal way to bring these new ideas to your prospects.

By solving client issues and delivering enhanced value, your reputation for producing results grows. Think of this as brand building. This in turn will make it easier to attract additional clients.

Your job isn't over just because you've won the sale. In the next chapter, we'll look at how to successfully manage this new relationship — and keep your clients happy — after you've closed the deal.

Key Takeaways

- A seller's reputation for producing results is the single most important selection criteria.

- Sellers overestimate the importance of price in the selection process.

- A good reputation can overcome the incumbent's advantage of having an existing relationship with the client.

- Educating the client and offering new perspectives is important to closing the sale.

- A strong strategic brand, driven by content marketing, offers a new model for success.

CHAPTER 7
Build Buyer Loyalty

W e've talked a lot about what it takes to get in front of prospects and then win new business. What about keeping that business? What does it take to turn new clients into long-term clients who not only reward you with repeat business but also refer you to their peers? What makes clients stay with you, and what causes them to leave?

We know from our research that the number one reason clients stay and the number two reason they leave are actually the same — do sellers do what they say they'll do? Do they make good on their promises?

We'll introduce the data in a moment. But think about where you are in the relationship when you start thinking about client loyalty. You've overcome some significant hurdles. You've captured prospects' attention by helping them understand that your firm is well positioned to solve their problem (recall the "relevancy gap" from Chapter 4). And as we learned in Chapter 6, you've managed to turn them from a prospect into a client by winning first on reputation, and then by demonstrating your ability to solve problems like theirs.

Never let the client set expectations or decide what promise you'll be keeping.

Yet sealing the deal does not give you license to sit back and relax with mojito in hand. You have to deliver on your promise throughout the engagement. And your ability to actually do this rides on how effectively you manage your client's expectations. Never let the client set those expectations or decide what promise you'll be keeping.

Our research shows just how important it is to deliver on your promises. To get an idea of what drives buyers to give sellers business, we first asked buyers to rank the likelihood that they would still be using their current service provider in 2-3 years, well after most projects or contracts are completed.

The results show that just over 71% strongly believe (answered with a 9 or a 10 score) they will be working with their current firm in 2-3 years and about 7% are very unlikely (responded with a score of 6 or less) to continue the relationship at that point. The remaining 21%, those who responded with a 7 or 8, could move in either direction.

Figure 7.1. Buyer Loyalty Rating Over 2-3 Years

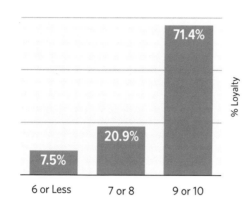

We then followed up by asking buyers to identify the driving forces behind their responses. The number one reason buyers gave for continuing the relationship was that their professional services provider actually did what they said they would do. In short, they delivered on their promise (see Figure 7.2 below).

Figure 7.2. Factors Influencing Loyalty

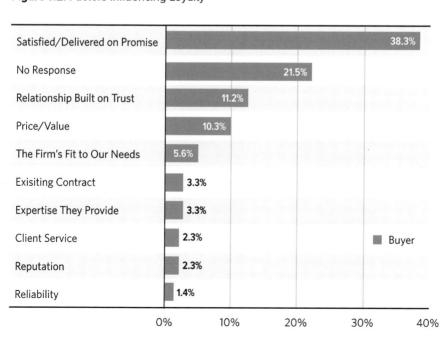

To be sure, there are other drivers of buyer loyalty, some very pragmatic (contractual agreements) and some more subjective (relationships). And recall from Chapter 6 the number one thing buyers are trying to avoid: sellers who don't deliver on their promises (22%). The lesson here is clear: The best way to lose loyalty is to not do what you say you will.

> The number one reason buyers gave for continuing the relationship was that their professional services provider actually did what they said they would do.

Now, what each firm promises will be different. But as we mentioned above, the key is to promise something that rings true to your brand. It must both be a goal you can achieve and be something that makes sense to the marketplace because of who you are, who your clients are and what types of services you associate with your brand.

This is where the firm that attempts to be all things to all people fails. It's nearly impossible to build a coherent brand around the promise of providing varied services to a broad audience at a high level of quality. Instead, your brand promise should speak to a clearly defined client segment — a concept so simple that both your buyers and your internal team can wrap their minds around it and articulate it. This clarity of purpose can have a profound and positive impact on your business development efforts.

Industry Differences

As we dug a little deeper into the data on buyer loyalty, we found an interesting pattern — when we break out the question of likelihood of working with the same provider in 2-3 years, buyer loyalty is different across industries. For example, 2- to 3-year loyalty is over 70% for both accounting/financial services and A/E/C services, but only 44% for both management consulting and technology services.

Figure 7.3. Buyer Loyalty Over 2-3 Years

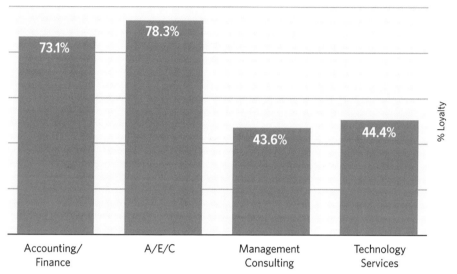

The reward of repeat business can be partially attributed to the fact that firms providing accounting and A/E/C services tend to have ongoing or recurring projects that more naturally translate into long-term relationships. On the other hand, the highly specific, contractual nature of many technology and management consulting projects can make ongoing relationships harder to establish.

Buyer loyalty is very different across industries.

This means that it is important that all firms, especially those in the management consulting and technology services areas, emphasize the ongoing relevance and value of their services. You must connect your services to your clients' ongoing business priorities.

How do you earn the unbridled loyalty of your clients? First, don't overpromise. That way you are in a position to do what you say you'll do. And second, don't fail to make it clear that your services are important to your clients' larger business objectives. Accomplish these tasks, and you'll capture the hearts — and long-term respect — of your clients.

Key Takeaways

- Client loyalty is most heavily impacted by your ability to deliver on your promises.

- Don't overpromise or leave client expectations to chance.

- Some industries are more likely to have long-term clients because of the recurring nature of their services (e.g., preparing tax paperwork).

- It is important to reinforce the connections between your service and your clients' important business priorities.

CASE STUDY

MicroLink: Developing Relationships that Last

an HP Autonomy company

Northern Virginia-based technology service provider MicroLink works with an assortment of vendors, including other technology specialists and marketing vendors. Jim Ferguson, VP of Corporate Development and Mark Bruininga, VP of Information Management, offer sellers a few tips for building robust, ongoing relationships with buyers.

Partners in the community

"Many sellers are wired to sell constantly," explains Ferguson. "They're too transaction-oriented and end up killing the relationship."

In Ferguson's opinion, long-term relationships aren't built on transactions alone. If every interaction between the two companies is about spending money, that's not a real relationship. In contrast, if the seller has a genuine interest in their client and isn't concerned only with selling the next project, there's an opportunity to forge a sustained, robust connection.

Responding to needs

For engagements lasting six months or longer, MicroLink prefers to deal with providers who are willing to work on a lasting relationship. According to Bruininga, "The companies that stay around the longest with us are the ones that demonstrate flexibility. How rapidly can they respond to new requirements and needs? How quickly can they make corrections?"

As a professional services provider you must work to understand the pain points of your prospect — and adjust course accordingly. Help them frame the problem and work together to pin down the exact issues and best approach. Once you've identified the problem, you must prove that you are both capable and flexible enough to execute the suggested approach.

MicroLink's challenges as a buyer aren't unique. Many purchasers struggle with the same hurdles and look to connect with sellers who are willing to develop a relationship and truly understand their business. Could you be more flexible? Could you help educate your prospects earlier in the process? The way you respond to these questions can have implications on your success.

CHAPTER 8
Expand the Relationship

Y ou've closed the client sale and you're about to embark on what promises to be a thriving working relationship. Your brand has served you well. You rode your reputation and visibility to the top of the client's list of potential providers.

Presumably, you are determined to deliver on the promises you made as you pursued the sale. That's a great start. As we have seen from our data, the top driver of buyer loyalty is keeping your word.

But now you're playing under different rules. The factors that won you the account — your reputation, your visibility, your skill at crafting a model for success — won't be enough to keep this new relationship flourishing. Now that you're the chosen firm, your clients expect you to deliver. To expand this relationship, you'll have to keep asking yourself a familiar question — even if the answer seems to be ever changing:

"What do my clients really want from me?"

Tell Me What You Value

As humans, our relationships are constantly evolving. What initially attracts us to someone is often quite different than what we come to value over time. As it turns out, this is also true with buyer-seller relationships in a professional services context. What attracts a company to a firm is not necessarily what they value most as the relationship evolves.

Reputations *sell*. Skills and expertise *prove*.

Shifting Priorities

We can see this evolution in priorities in Figure 8.1. We found that above all other criteria, most buyers — 68% — value a firm's specialized skills and expertise.

Figure 8.1. Top Values and Benefits of Service

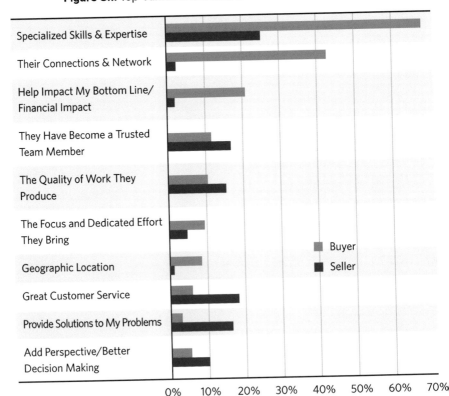

Wait a minute. Didn't we show you research in Chapter 6 that insisted buyers are swayed by different factors, like your good reputation?

Indeed we did. But now you are no longer in the marketing and selling phase of the relationship. Remember, most buyers are not well equipped to evaluate skills and expertise. So they tend to look at other factors, such as reputation, to compensate for their inability to gauge expertise. After all, a firm with a good reputation clearly has sufficient skills to do the job well.

But now that you have won the sale, your specialized skills and expertise are exactly what the client values most. Clients want to see that their issues are being addressed. It's not hard to understand. Reputations sell. Skills and expertise deliver.

Too often, sellers don't pay careful attention to the evolution of their partnership with buyers. They assume buyers will always seek the same thing. But these priorities can shift at varying points in your relationship.

Over time, buyers come to value factors that directly impact their business: skills and expertise (68%), peer networking, especially in the A/E/C industry (42%) and the financial impact a seller exerts on the buyer's bottom line (21%).

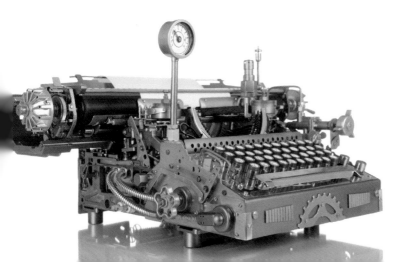

Unfortunately, sellers often underestimate the importance of these components. At the same time, sellers can overestimate factors like being a trusted team member and the quality of their work. Sure, all of these aspects are important. But they aren't crucial to buyers at this point in the relationship.

What's the lesson here? Make sure your client recognizes the expertise you bring to their project, as well as any impact you may have on their bottom line. If you can demonstrate that you do your work exceptionally well and can tangibly help their business, your firm will be well positioned to expand the relationship, get more repeat business and receive more referrals.

Why don't clients rate quality higher? Does that mean quality doesn't matter? Of course, you want to deliver the best work you can. But clients don't emphasize it as much because, as we've mentioned before, most of them aren't in a position to assess the quality of your work. They simply don't have the technical knowledge to determine whether your work is as good as it can be.

> Make sure your client recognizes the expertise you are bringing to their project, as well as any impact you may have on their bottom line.

Think of the accountant who prepares your taxes. When you receive your tax return to sign and put in the mail you can check it for obvious mistakes. But most of us simply don't have the knowledge to determine if the return takes advantage of every deduction and wrinkle in the tax law. Instead, you look to your accountant's reputation (and perhaps whether or not last year's tax bill was a surprise) for reassurance. It's no different for most professional services buyers.

Getting More Business

Professional services firms love to get additional business from their clients. And over 79% of buyers would like to purchase more services from their current provider (see Figure 8.2). But despite these seemingly ideal conditions, clients often go elsewhere for services that the provider offered (remember Daniel and Maxine in Chapter 1?).

Figure 8.2. Buyers Interested in New Services

As you can see in Figure 8.3, a whopping 48% of buyers admit that, even as they seek more help from their sellers, they don't always know the scope of the services they provide. Clearly, opportunities are being left on the table. Buyers want to buy more. But most professional services firms are doing a poor job of telling their clients what their firms have to offer.

Figure 8.3. Are Buyers Aware of Services?

How to Market to Your Clients

Your clients want new services. They are open to your ideas and innovations. They're just waiting for you to knock on their door and show them how you can help address their key priorities.

But what's the best way to offer a client something new?

Figure 8.4. How New Services Should be Offered

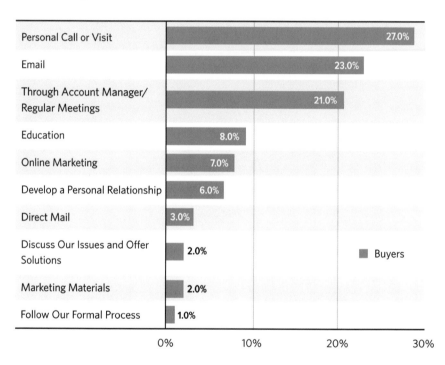

As you can see in Figure 8.4, buyers said they liked the personal touch. From the buyer's perspective, the best marketing strategies involve personal relationships (27%), personal emails (23%) and direct contact with an account manager (21%). Clearly, these are all natural parts of a good account management process.

Key Takeaways

- After you win the sale, clients' expectations change.

- Most clients are not qualified to evaluate skills and expertise. Nor are they good at judging quality of work.

- Instead, clients look for evidence that you are bringing specialized skills and expertise to the project, as well as bottom-line results.

- Buyers want new services from their provider. But they don't always know what you can do for them. If you don't tell them, they may go elsewhere.

- The best ways to market to your clients is through a personal call, a face-to-face visit or by email. You can also let them know during regular meetings or account interaction.

CASE STUDY

Standing Out from the Crowd: How to Sell to a Public Institution

Northern Virginia Community College (NOVA) is one of the largest educational institutions in the country, serving over 78,000 students and employing approximately 3,000 faculty and staff. As Chief Administrative Officer (CAO) at NOVA, Tony Bansal oversees the procurement of all college goods and services, including capital budgets associated with new construction and maintenance of existing facilities at six campuses and nine centers. We went to Tony for the inside scoop on how firms win the bid.

In institutions, procurement follows procedure

Like many institutions, NOVA follows a rigorous procedure for procurement. "We sit down and try to understand our own needs," says Tony. "How can we accomplish what we need, and why do we need it?" NOVA then develops an extensive statement of work, which has rich details of the specific tasks and activities expected from the vendor. The statement of work also provides the context within which the services have to be provided and the desired outcome at the end of the assignment. NOVA's procurement department finalizes the procurement requirements and is responsible for sending out RFPs and collecting vendors' proposals and bids. A selection committee with members from different disciplines, both academic and administrative, is formed to make the final selection. The committee reads through proposals, weeding out providers who can't meet or don't seem to understand the college's specific needs.

How is your organization unique?
At this point, vendors are winnowed down to a small pool of competitors, all of whom could probably handle the job. Then comes the moment of truth, when Tony interviews short-listed prospects one-by-one.

"In the interview process," Tony says, "it's a given that you're knowledgeable and can do the work. But what's unique about you?" To win the contract, a vendor needs to stand out. The presentation is an opportunity for service providers to show how they can provide something more or different than competitors.

"You have to make sure you have something to sell," Tony says. "Something unique — process, methodology, software, something where you have a unique advantage or price."

Help solve a problem
For NOVA, the best service providers demonstrate a thorough understanding of both the higher education industry and the problem the college has identified. According to Tony, providers need to remember that "each organization is different, and the issues are going to be different. Their understanding of our issue needs to be from *our* point of view."

At NOVA, cost is less important than proving you're somehow better or different than the competition, demonstrating that you understand the college's needs, and showing how you'll help solve a problem. For firms hoping to sell to NOVA, Tony advises, "read up, learn as much as you can about the industry. Your solutions need to be well thought-out and must work in the client's context."

CHAPTER 9
Get the Referral

The most beneficial buyer-seller relationship is the one that keeps on giving. As we've learned, when sellers nurture and manage the relationship with the buyer by delivering on their promises, proving value through skill and expertise and continually offering a spectrum of services that meets the buyer's needs, more often than not the buyer rewards them with repeat business over time. But that's not the end of the story.

One often overlooked but critical component of the relationship is encouraging the client to make referrals. In fact, we often think of referrals as the lifeblood of professional services firms. Why? First, referred clients cost little or nothing to cultivate, close more quickly and are usually easier to manage. Second, remember what we learned in Chapter 5 — referrals are the number one way buyers discover sellers with whom they do not have an established relationship (see Figure 5.1). Yet our research shows that while most buyers are willing to refer their seller, very few sellers are in the habit of formally securing those referrals, potentially leaving business on the table.

The Role of Referrals

Buyers turn to their peers to find a provider. "Who has the best reputation? Who has the most proven expertise? Who is the best at solving the problem?" Chances are, referrals fueled more of your own growth than any other marketing channel.

Winning new business through referrals plays such a pivotal role in a firm's growth that we dedicated a portion of our research specifically to the subject. We started by asking buyers how likely they were to refer their service providers. We found that the vast majority are very willing to refer. In fact, 69% of buyers are very willing to recommend their service providers (responding with a score of 9 or 10).

Figure 9.1 Probability Buyers Would Refer Sellers

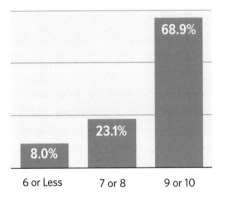

Getting the Referral

Next, we asked the buyers if they had in fact referred their provider. While 74% said they had indeed referred their provider at some point in time, over a quarter said they hadn't.

A 26% non-referral rate may not sound bad. But the kicker is the reason for those lost referrals. The vast majority of buyers (72%) didn't refer their service providers simply because they hadn't been asked!

Figure 9.2. Why Buyers Haven't Referred

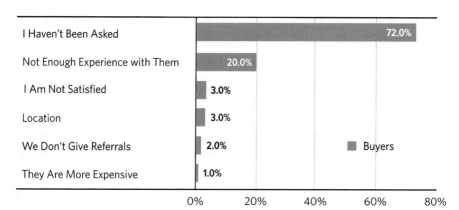

I Haven't Been Asked	72.0%
Not Enough Experience with Them	20.0%
I Am Not Satisfied	3.0%
Location	3.0%
We Don't Give Referrals	2.0%
They Are More Expensive	1.0%

Only 20% of buyers who hadn't referred said they were insufficiently experienced with the service provider to refer them, and a mere 3% reported dissatisfaction with the service. Because no one had asked these buyers about their service providers, they hadn't made any referrals. Clearly, there's an opportunity to improve referral rates. The challenge here is getting people — anybody in the marketplace, not just your clients — to talk about you when you're not in the room so that when people need services like those you provide your firm is the one that comes to mind. And when these folks are ready to buy, they'll approach your clients for validation.

> 69% of buyers are very willing to recommend their service providers

But how do you lay a foundation for conversations like these?

Getting the Right Referral

To help people make the case for your firm, you need a powerful brand. Strong brands yield strong referrals. Brands that rise to the top are clearly differentiated and have relevant, easy-to-understand messaging — a clear story about their value proposition that sets them apart from the sea of competitors.

Because no one had asked these buyers about their service providers, they hadn't made any referrals.

Conversely, a firm with a weak brand is difficult to describe in compelling terms. As a result, these firms are less memorable and tend to receive fewer referrals. And when they are referred, it is often to the wrong audiences. What a waste!

The importance of brand to the referral cannot be overstated. Think about it — many of your own clients don't know what you can do for them (recall the painful truth that many buyers don't know what the seller's services are), so how can you expect your clients to know what you can do for others?

Getting Others to Ask

In addition to building a strong brand, you can provide some important resources to help prospects seek a referral from your buyers:

- **Publicize your clients:** The value in listing your clients on your website or your collateral far outweighs the risk that a competitor will swoop in and take them away (a common, if misinformed, concern). Making your client list visible creates credibility with prospective buyers when a direct referral isn't a possibility. We recognize, of course, that some industries and circumstance require client confidentiality that make this option impossible.

- **Showcase your success:** Case studies allow buyers to slip into the shoes of your clients. They help prospects understand how you've solved problems similar to theirs before. Press releases highlight your firm's successes, awards and other achievements. These are all things that might interest referral sources, so you want to be sure they are easy to find and access on your website and elsewhere.

> The importance of brand to the referral cannot be overstated.

In Chapter 4, we learned that after turning to peers for a referral, online search is the third most mentioned action buyers will take when looking for a provider. Whether buyers are using online search to find service provider candidates or to gather additional information on firms they're already considering, most buyers are going online at some point in the decision-making process, and they're judging your reputation on what they see and read. So take your website seriously. It is your single most important marketing tool.

Additionally, sometimes it may be useful to ask your clients for a referral directly. While not covered in our findings, it's a common and viable strategy that you should consider when appropriate.

Buyers value a firm's reputation for producing results much more than sellers think. So sellers that don't consciously develop their reputation and visibility (that is, their brand) will be at a disadvantage. The next section of this book will lay out specific tools and strategies for building your brand so that you can become well known and respected in your marketplace.

Key Takeaways

- Most clients are more than willing to make a referral.

- Most referrals are made in response to a request for a referral.

- The biggest reason clients don't make the referral is that no one has asked them for one, not because they are dissatisfied.

- You can increase referrals by increasing the profile of your clients by listing them on your website and featuring them in case studies (so they get asked more often).

- A strong brand makes it easier for people to refer new business to your firm.

PART III:
Building a Better Brand

Know your edge. Make sure the world knows it, too.

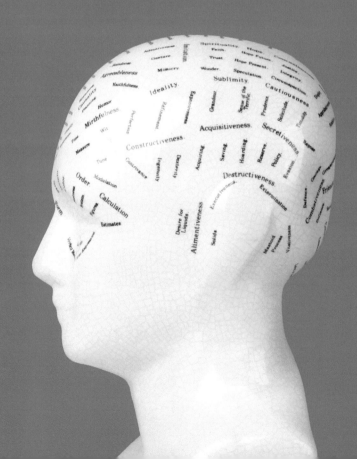

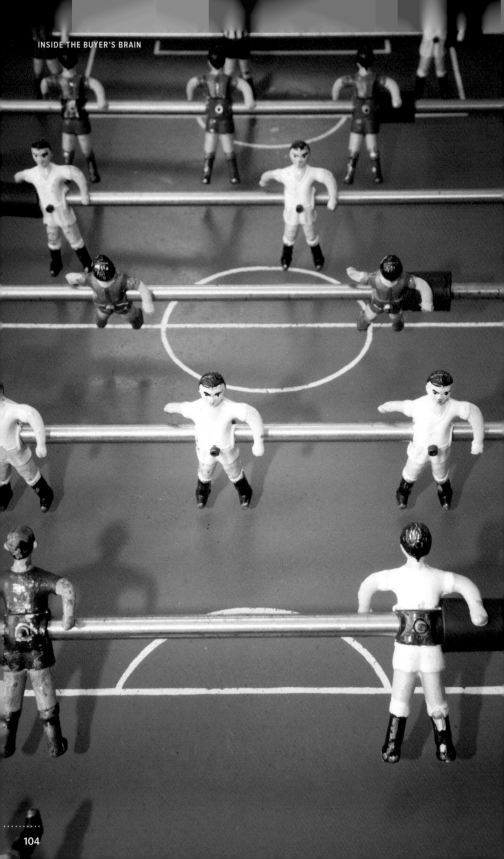

CHAPTER 10
Get the Strategy Right

O kay. You've taken a long, hard look into the minds of your buyers. You've learned about all the things your firm should do to connect with your prospects, close the sale, expand the relationship and encourage referrals. But how does your firm build its reputation and visibility? How do you sustain growth into the future?

The answer is branding. And that's the focus of the next three chapters. A strong brand speaks to your prospective clients' needs, creates an emotional connection with buyers and conveys your competitive advantage to the right marketplace. It also helps solidify your internal culture and attract the right kind of employees.

We like to break the branding process down into three parts:

- Getting the strategy right

- Crafting your branding tools

- Building your brand

In this chapter, we focus on getting the strategy right. That involves developing the twin pillars of a strong branding strategy: positioning and messaging.

Professional Services Research vs. Consumer Research: What's the Difference?

By now, you know your professional services firm needs to understand both itself and the wider marketplace. If you're already familiar with consumer research companies, you might wonder whether there's any difference between professional services and consumer research.

In short, they're two completely different beasts.

Because each school of research deals with completely different types of deliverables — services versus products, for the most part — they use distinct methodologies to achieve different goals. Consumer research usually needs to understand a very broad group of buyers. That means big, general samples that strive to identify common emotional responses to relatively small purchases, usually by posing simple, closed-ended questions. "Would you buy Detergent X?" This is a simple yes or no question, and the answer may be a matter of impulse.

This methodology makes sense for consumer products, but professional services have different needs and processes. If you're selling financial services, for example, you need to elicit a very specific response from CFOs — they have to trust that you won't sink their company. And you can be sure they're not going to make an impulse buy. For this reason, professional services research uses smaller, highly targeted sample groups and open-ended questioning to paint a detailed picture of the facts that matter most: the dynamics of your specific marketplace and the precise services that you provide to your clients and prospects.

Know Thyself

If your branding is built upon a distorted view of your marketplace or your firm, even the slickest logo or most stunning brochure won't save you. It's absolutely essential to do due diligence on yourself and your audiences before you start your makeover. Fortunately, all it takes is a little research.

> A strong brand speaks to your prospective clients' needs, creates an emotional connection with buyers, and conveys your competitive advantage to the right marketplace.

At the beginning of this book, we showed you that high growth, high profit firms conduct regular research. Now, think about what you could learn from the following groups:

- **Internal staff:** What does your management team think about your brand? How about your staff? Contrasting these perceptions with those of outside audiences can be very revealing and help persuade your team to think about themselves and your clients differently.

- **Current clients:** Your existing clients can offer insights into what it's really like to work with you, perhaps exposing blind spots or unrecognized strengths. They help you examine your process from another perspective.

- **Former clients:** If you want to understand your operating weaknesses and figure out how to create more robust relationships, past clients can be an invaluable resource.

- **Prospects:** Potential buyers can illuminate your brand's current perceptions in the open marketplace — how you compare to the competition and what makes your firm special. This is an even more critical audience to research if you're looking to shift or expand your target audience.

- **Lost prospects:** The ones who got away can help you understand the hard truths — what buyers see as your weaknesses.

- **Influencers:** Analysts, bloggers and community leaders can be powerful shapers of opinion in many industries. Knowing how they perceive your firm can be very valuable.

- **Competitors:** If you want a clear picture of both your status in the marketplace and what opportunities aren't being addressed, you may want to research your competition. This also means finding out who your clients and prospects consider your competition to be. Usually there is only about a 25% overlap with your own list of competitors.

- **Prospective employees:** Surveying prospective employees will help you understand how well your brand positions you to compete for top talent. Are potential team members attracted to your brand? Do they understand the services your firm provides?

This sort of research helps you understand your clients' real challenges, how well positioned you are to address those challenges, who they consider your competitors and how aware they are of the services you offer.

The easiest way to collect this data is to send out a written or online survey. But this approach doesn't encourage people to volunteer experiences not covered in the survey. A better approach is to interview people in each group, either in person or by phone.

To get the most honest and useful information out of these audiences, you will need to bring in an impartial third party to conduct the interviews — someone who can guarantee the responders' anonymity. Negative comments can be extraordinarily valuable, but many clients simply won't volunteer these experiences to you directly for fear of hurting your feelings or damaging the relationship. Some clients may also withhold praise for fear that it might encourage you to raise your fees.

Once you get your research down, you can craft your brand strategy. This is not a logo or visual styling. Rather, it's the way you define yourself in the context of the marketplace. And to get there, you first need to be clear about what makes you different — your differentiators.

Knowing the Difference

You need to be able to prove that you can and will deliver service that matters to your audience. That means building your reputation around characteristics that are true, meaningful to your audience and supportable.

Take Mazuma, a British accounting firm. Mazuma targets a young audience working from small or home offices. They organize clients' financial papers themselves, collecting all the relevant materials by mailing clients a purple collection envelope every month. Mazuma's fee is monthly, too. These probably aren't the particulars you imagined when you read "British accounting firm" — Mazuma stands out with a unique audience focus, process and pricing model.

Once you get your research down, you can craft your brand strategy.

Too many firms claim they are different, when in fact potential clients see no distinction between them and look-alike firms. For instance, let's consider the statement, "Our clients are always satisfied." Let's say, for the sake of argument, that this statement is true, backed up by an in-depth customer satisfaction survey. If it's not meaningful to your audience, it doesn't matter. New buyers are looking for you to demonstrate that you can solve the problems they're facing right now.

So what makes for a good differentiator?

- **Industry specialization:** Some successful brands choose to highlight their industry specialization, leveraging an insider status in a given industry or related set of industries. For example, a CPA firm might work exclusively with technology firms.

- **Client demographic:** You might serve clients primarily over the age 65. Is there a particular type or group of buyer that you're particularly well-suited to serve?

- **Specialized staff:** One of our clients in the technology industry hires only computer science PhDs. Everyone claims to have a peerless team, but if you can actually prove it, that can be a fantastic differentiator.

- **Specialized services:** Do you offer a service that others do not? Or do you specialize in a service when others simply include it as one of many?

- **Business model:** Do you have a novel way of offering or pricing your service? Perhaps others offer service by the hour while you offer it for a fixed price. Or maybe you sell it by subscription rather than project invoice.

- **Geographic focus:** Are you national where others are local? Or vice versa? While less powerful than in the past, a geographic differentiator can work in some situations.

Like Mazuma, you can take these differentiator categories and combine them to identify a unique and powerful competitive advantage. With that advantage isolated, you're poised to lay down the foundations of your firm's strategy: a positioning statement and a marketing architecture.

Positioning for an Edge

One of your most powerful branding tools is a positioning statement, a brief paragraph or two that distills your brand into a few pithy sentences. This is the story of your firm, succinctly told: what defines you, whom you serve, what you offer them and how you see yourself.

Your brand positioning is the product of your key competitive differences and your aspirations for the firm.

Let's take a look at a positioning statement for an architecture firm (for the sake of this example, we've changed the firm's name):

Agents of Change

Newco Architects is shaping the way educational, correctional and civic buildings are designed and built. As pioneers of green design, we're committed to creating functional and sustainable communities. And with a strong reputation for delivering on our promises, we're transforming the public-sector built environment, one project at a time. At Newco, we find the inspiration to create more beautiful, useful and responsible public spaces in the opportunities of tomorrow.

Your brand positioning is the product of your key competitive differences and your aspirations for the firm. A positioning statement should be relevant to all of your brand's audiences and represent all of its services. It is by definition a high level summary of your firm. But it is also true, relevant and supportable, building on the differentiators you've identified. Newco affirms a specialty in educational, correctional, and civic buildings as well as an emphasis on green design. These are specific claims that they can support and follow through on for clients.

A word of caution: Don't let your brand be dictated by your competitors, either by rushing to ape them or defining yourself in opposition to them. Do your homework and find a place where you have a competitive advantage. Successful positioning identifies your firm's edge, claims a space in the marketplace and helps you own it.

Your positioning is an internal document, a story about yourself for yourself, but it provides guidance for your firm's messaging. If you can explain your firm to yourself — its value proposition, key differentiators, market position and particular ambitions — then you're prepared to talk about it in the marketplace.

Strategic Messaging

We tend to communicate differently depending on our audience and context. For example, you're generally not going to talk to a stranger in line at the grocery store quite the same way you talk to a childhood friend. In brand communications, you must cater your message to specific audiences. Those groups we looked to for research — potential clients, influencers, prospective employees and the rest — have different needs and interests, and they often require different messaging.

That's where your messaging architecture comes in. This document identifies your target audiences and tailors your message (based on your positioning) to each of them. These audiences will likely include the usual suspects, such as employees and prospective buyers, but your messaging architecture might also address specific industries, segments or roles within your target groups.

We tend to communicate differently depending on our audience and context.

A strong messaging architecture consists of three parts:

- **Key messages:** These are audience-specific messages rooted firmly in your positioning statement, but addressing the interests or needs of the audience in greater detail.

- **Objections:** If you identify each group's likely arguments or concerns up front, you prepare yourself to address them consistently and effectively when they come up with buyers.

- **Counter-arguments:** Your messaging should prepare you to respond to those likely points of resistance with appropriate evidence such as formal research, case studies, testimonials or publications.

A solid messaging architecture marshals proof points and targeted messaging to carry your brand mindfully into the marketplace. In conjunction with your positioning statement, carefully crafted messaging captures your brand strategy. These will be powerful resources as you prepare your branding toolkit and write content for your website and marketing collateral. And of course, they are essential to helping your team talk about your firm in a way that sets you apart in the marketplace.

Now that we have our strategy down, let's look at the tools we'll use to carry it out. See you in the next chapter.

Key Takeaways

- Branding lets your buyers know that your firm can and will meet their needs.

- Strong brands are built on attributes of your firm that are specific, demonstrable and true. But that's not enough.

- Carving a unique space for yourself in the marketplace helps you create a truly distinct brand.

- A positioning statement is a document that acts as an internal guidepost, succinctly defining your position in the marketplace — including your unique value, attributes and audience.

- A messaging architecture tailors your message specifically to particular audiences, helping you to communicate differently and appropriately with potential buyers, prospective employees, existing clients and more.

CASE STUDY

The 7 Desires of Service Buyers: Tips from a Master Purchaser

 Vendor Centric

"Service trumps everything else," says Tom Rogers, founder and CEO of Vendor Centric. "When I send an email to our IT firm and say we need a new email account, and they take care of it right away plus ask if I need anything else — they'll stay a long time."

Vendor Centric helps national trade associations design, build and manage group purchasing cooperatives. Tom drew on his ten years of experience in vendor management to explain what service buyers look for in a partner:

1. Focus: Firms that try to sell too many services in too many industries tend to lose out against firms that focus on a niche. Tom suggests specializing in either a specific service or a particular industry market where your firm has a competitive edge.

2. Expertise: "Qualified vendors understand the industry, provide solutions, and put together product offerings that get to the needs of the marketplace," Tom says. Sellers have to do the research before pursuing a sale; if you don't understand the client industry, it's hard to offer the right solution.

3. Understanding: Many sales reps jump straight into their products and services, but this typically offers solutions to the wrong problems. Take the time to identify buyers' specific challenges and needs. Ask appropriate questions, then listen.

4. Results: Find past cases where client needs aligned with your current prospect's situation and identify measurable results, such as cost savings or revenue increases. If you've solved similar problems in another situation, you have evidence you can do it again.

5. Guidance: "The initial focus should be around education," explains Tom. "Educate the buyer throughout the process and help them to realize how your service may fit the need." By guiding prospects through an area they may not fully comprehend, you can build trust and form a relationship.

6. Account Management: Buyers want to know that day-to-day communication will be straightforward, services will be delivered on time, and invoices will be easy to understand. If you commit to stellar communication up front, buyers take note.

7. Price: According to Tom, price is a secondary concern. Cheaper isn't always better. Buyers are more likely to choose a firm that fully understands their specific problems, even if it means paying premium prices.

Buyers look for vendors that take the time to understand their challenges, have a proven ability to provide solutions and follow through. Take a look at your sales and business development team — are they providing what buyers really desire?

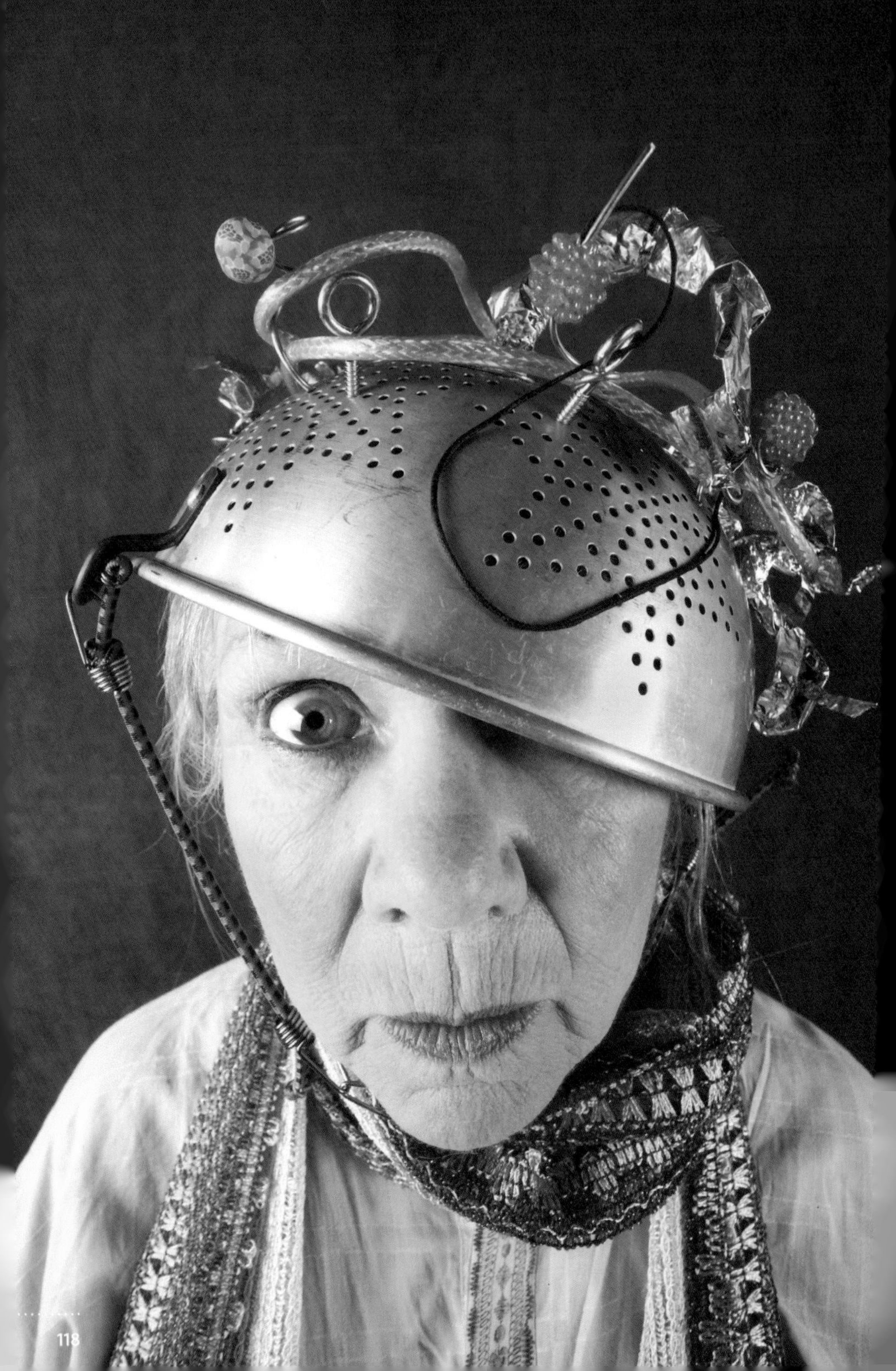

CHAPTER 11
The Tools You'll Need

Once you've nailed down your strategy, it's time to put together your brand building toolbox. Branding tools are the techniques you use to build your visibility or reputation, and they have to be informed at every step by your market positioning and messaging architecture. These tools carry your strategy boldly into the marketplace. Some are obvious: logo design, color palette, typography and other visual elements that most people associate with the word "brand."

Other techniques aren't so obvious, nor very common. But if you can take advantage of these tools, the ones that are often the secret weapons of high growth firms, you might start to feel a little sorry for the rest of the pack.

Building the Brand

Let's start with the basics. Remember to build logically: if you're going to make any adjustments to your firm's name, for example, you're going to want to do that before you start assembling your tools.

First up: logo and tagline. Your logo should be memorable and immediately recognizable, with a visual style that distinguishes your firm from your key competitors. A symbol, while not required, can help people recognize your brand. A tagline serves as your logo's partner in action. It can clarify the services you provide, bolster your positioning or express some other key facet of your brand. Some firms have taglines, others don't — because different brands have different descriptive needs. But a tagline provides another way to communicate important information about your firm.

Strong branding techniques raise your visibility or enhance your reputation. But the most powerful tools do both at the same time.

Once your logo and tagline are in place, you can begin building out your suite of marketing collateral tools. These may include stationery, email templates, brochures, PowerPoint templates, sales sheets and proposal formats, to name just a few. These materials create a unified identity that presents your firm in its best light at every step.

You may want to develop guidelines for your visual brand, as well. Brand guidelines help govern the implementation of your brand in a consistent, orderly and ongoing way, answering questions such as:

- How do I use our logo consistently across a range of media?

- Which typefaces should I use on firm materials?

- What are our corporate colors?

- How do I use photographs in our materials?

If you want to maintain a consistent visual brand over time — especially if you have multiple offices — guidelines are an invaluable investment.

So you've got a unified set of materials sitting in your toolbox, ready to communicate your brand wherever you take it. But what about those other tools — the secret weapons of high growth firms? Well, they are right out in the open, and they never stop working for you.

Tools for a Visible Reputation

Strong branding techniques can raise your visibility or enhance your reputation. But the most powerful tools do both at the same time.

As we've already shown you, buyers want to be educated. They want information that is useful and relevant to their needs, right here and right now. If you can provide that education, you demonstrate your expertise while raising your profile. How can you get there? Consider developing several of the following brand tools to highlight your firm's authority and educate your audience.

New (and shared) industry research: You're ideally placed not only to conduct research on the industry you serve, but also to share it openly. Help clients and potential clients alike answer big questions in their fields, and they'll look to you as a driven and knowledgeable leader.

A specialized conference: Speaking at conferences (and sponsoring them) is a traditional strategy for raising your brand's visibility, but you can take this tack a bold step further by organizing a new conference. Just as you searched for your firm's unique competitive advantage, think about niches in your industry currently uncovered by any major conferences, niches that fall squarely in your area of expertise. Center your gathering on this specific topic. This can be a powerful way to announce your expertise to the marketplace.

The top book, by you: If you or someone in your firm has the expertise to write the book on your signature topic, then do it. This can be a demanding but highly rewarding investment. To encourage your clients and prospects to read it, keep the language simple and nontechnical. While you may want to take your book to a traditional publisher for the cachet that brings, don't forget about self-publishing your masterpiece as an e-book. You will have complete flexibility to offer some or all of it for free as part of a larger content marketing campaign. Today, self-published books have lost much of their second-class reputation and can be just as effective as their printed counterparts.

An industry newsletter people look forward to reading: A newsletter may seem traditional, but when supported by robust content it can be a compelling brand-builder. Avoid fluff and transparent self-promotion; instead, focus on your industry through the unique lens of your firm. The newsletter can also be a great tool for letting people know about the range of resources you offer.

Readers of newsletters want useful information. You can even be a little provocative so long as you truly believe what you say. Your newsletter may even help you lead the conversation in your industry.

> Use your tools the right way, and you can create a vibrant brand building cycle.

Your present and future Visible Expertsˢᴹ**:** A Visible Expertˢᴹ is a truly high-profile leader in your industry — one quoted in the media and sought out for speaking engagements. If you have individuals like this on your team, help support and develop their reputations. Your firm will share the glow, much as some universities benefit from their Nobel prize-winning faculty members. Cloud software platform vendor Heroku is a great example of this strategy: one of their Chief Architects, Yukihiro "Matz" Matsumoto, is revered by programmers worldwide for creating the Ruby programming language. Matz gives major talks on Ruby at Heroku's specialized cloud computing conferences — often to sold-out crowds.

Even if you don't have a superstar expert on staff, you can groom talented members of your team to assume this mantle in the future. Books, blogs, speaking engagements and savvy social media content can help raise the profile of your talented experts — and sharpen the reputation of your firm.

Your firm's story, now playing everywhere: For about the cost of a signature brochure, you can create an impressive video that speaks directly to your audience, telling your firm's story through the mouths of your clients and/or your Visible Experts℠. A well-told story — especially one that educates the viewer — will engage viewers in a way that written material simply can't. Video also appeals to those prospects who either prefer audio-visual content or don't have the time to read a lot of material.

A must-read blog: Like a newsletter, your blog can be a platform for your firm's singular take on its field of expertise. Think of your blog as an ongoing publication for your industry, like a magazine with topics and features that your clients will want to read. To attract qualified prospects over time, you'll want to incorporate SEO principles into your blogging strategy. By incrementally adding keyword-specific content to your blog, you'll be able to attract targeted search engine traffic — and develop a growing, interested readership.

Your blog is a great place to support other tools. For example, if you have Visible Experts℠ (present or future) on your team, share their knowledge on your blog. That raises the stature of the blog, which in turn may further expand the reach of your experts. Use your tools the right way, and you can create a vibrant brand-building cycle. But you have to commit to it, publishing well and often.

That brings us to your website: We can't overstate the importance of your website to your brand and your firm's ability to generate leads. Often, it's your first foot forward — the place that every one of your audiences is likely to visit to understand your services, process and positioning.

"But that's not a secret weapon," you might say. "Everybody knows you need a website." That's true enough — but there are websites and then there are *websites*. If you want to build a powerful brand in today's electronic marketplace, your site must become a lead-generating engine.

All of your branding tools — videos, books, blogs, conference announcements, screencasts and more — meet in your website. It is the place that interested people (many of whom will turn into quality leads) go to find new research, to check up on what your Visible Experts℠ are saying and to learn. When prospects see your website as a dynamic, relevant resource, you'll be well on your way to building a powerful brand.[1]

The Necessary Spectrum

Many of these top branding tools are ongoing commitments that require a blended skill set: talents as diverse as web development, video production, writing, audio engineering, print publication design, conference organization, e-book production — the list goes on. What's more, you'll need people who can do these things reliably and well. If you don't have the resources to produce these materials yourself, don't despair. Look for a qualified firm that offers the specific set of skills you need, or hire individual consultants to handle tasks that aren't suited for your internal team.

Next up: Using your tools to build your brand.

---

1 You can learn much more about high performance websites in our free book, *Online Marketing for Professional Services*.

Key Takeaways

- Your core branding tools must support your positioning statement and messaging architecture — and you have to build them in a logical order.

- Brand style guidelines can help you manage the consistent application of your visual brand over time.

- Some of the most powerful brand tools build your reputation and visibility at the same time by offering your target audience practical educational resources in your area of expertise.

- To create a full suite of contemporary branding tools, you're going to need a blended skill set of highly diverse talents.

CHAPTER 12
Build the Brand

t's show time. You've got a differentiating new logo and tagline. You have the tools and strategies you need to reach your buyers. You've got a website that is primed to generate new leads. In this chapter, we'll show you how to be everywhere your client is — using the content marketing model.

But first, you have to prepare your new brand for its first day on the job.

Ready for launch

In some ways, your brand launch is no different from the grand opening of a new store or restaurant. The real work will come later, but this is a fantastic opportunity to command the attention of your market and start off on the right foot.

Before you do anything else, introduce the brand internally. Your new branding is a proxy for your staff and the work that they do. A strong brand can really bolster employee morale and team cohesion, and an energetic team will be a powerful engine for the brand going forward. Get your employees familiar with the ins and outs of your brand. Introduce them to your positioning statement, messaging architecture, and brand guidelines.

And be sure to share key research findings with your staff to set the stage for the "why" behind your new brand. Work with your team until they can articulate your brand clearly, consistently and confidently. They will be your first line of brand advocates.

When you're ready to go public with your brand, make sure you have a rollout plan. This rollout plan should lay out the specifics of what you will do to communicate your brand to the world, how you will do it and when.

Your brand launch is an exciting milestone. But remember, this ain't the end. Your launch is the beginning of the real work and the real rewards — the steady and continuous effort of building your brand.

Before you do anything else, introduce the brand internally.

The Content Marketing Model

In our research, we asked buyers to identify the best ways to market to them. Figure 12.1 presents the top two results.

Figure 12.1. Top Ways Buyers Want to Be Marketed To

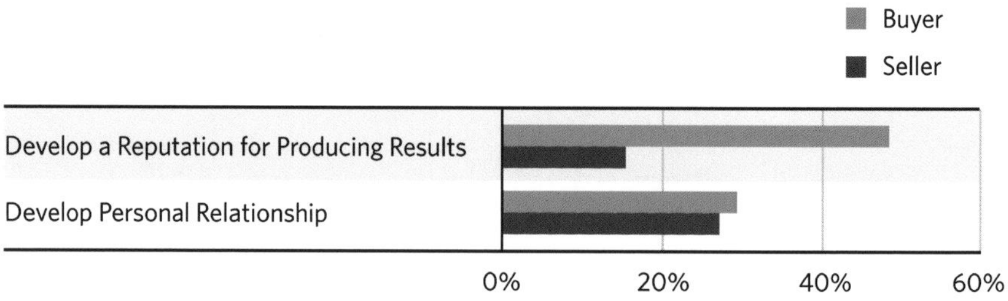

By a wide margin, professional services buyers reported that "developing a reputation for producing results" was the best way to market to them, far more effective than forging a personal relationship.

What's the takeaway? You need a brand that people want to recommend to friends and colleagues, a brand they feel they already know. The tools we discussed in the last chapter don't just give buyers something to search for online — they communicate enough about your expertise and approach that people feel they know you even if they haven't worked with you.

Work with your staff until they can articulate your brand clearly, consistently and confidently.

Here's an example. Let's say you're pretty new to the work force, and you mostly work from home. With tax season on the horizon, you go online and discover a freely available online guide to deducting your home office. It is written by a reputable-looking CPA firm. It appears to be thorough, useful and even a little funny. The home office guide directs you to a YouTube conference talk by the guide's author, whom you discover after a quick Google search is well known and respected in her field. If a friend comes to you asking about CPAs, we bet you'll remember that firm. And your friend won't have to take your word about the firm's expertise and style — he will have access to all of the same experiences you did.

To better understand this process, we developed a content marketing model (which we describe extensively in our book *Online Marketing for Professional Services*).

Figure 12.2. The Modern Content Marketing Model

1 Get the Strategy Right
2 Create
3 Promote
4 Nurture & Convert
5 Analyze & Adjust

By now, the first steps should be familiar. Getting your strategy right provides a foundation for your content marketing — and your branding — in your firm's strengths and opportunities. Once you've got your strategy nailed down, you can get to work creating relevant content.

Use short-form content such as blog posts to attract new visitors and encourage previous visitors to return to your website. These pieces should be free and easy to access, with no registration required. They are designed to establish trust and demonstrate your expertise. To turn these readers into leads, you will want to develop in-depth educational content, such as e-books, webinars or guides. Because they offer more apparent value, many visitors will be willing to exchange basic contact information for these longer pieces. If your audience feels like they've gotten their money's worth (or in this case, their registration's worth), they'll trust you even more.

CRM—Automating the Lead Generation Process

You should promote your lead-nurturing content on your website, where you can use offers, forms and (if you have one) your client relationship management (CRM) software to create a highly automated and effective lead generation system. A CRM will help you organize and track your engagements with clients on an extremely fine-grained level. CRM tools are particularly effective for synchronizing client engagements that may occur across many different areas of your company. This gives your sales team, for instance, a comprehensive view of interactions between a client and your firm's technical support.

Some of the most commonly used platforms include Infusionsoft, Microsoft Dynamics, HubSpot, SugarCRM and Salesforce. Major CRM tools vary in sophistication, ease of use and the range of capabilities they offer. For example, Salesforce offers a system that's accessible anywhere and provides a broad suite of services, supporting campaigns from organizations like GE and Wells Fargo. Depending on their size and needs, some companies require this wide range of functionality, while others find that they need services with a particular focus. Infusionsoft, for instance, specializes in helping small businesses manage their client relationships. In order to find the most effective tool, you should measure the strengths and weaknesses of available tools against your specific needs.

Keep your registration forms as short and minimal as possible. In some cases an email address alone is sufficient to build a list, though other information (such as name and company) will give you more to work with. The fewer fields you require, the more people will complete the form.

To turn these readers into leads, you will want to develop in-depth educational content, such as e-books, webinars or guides.

Once you have collected even the most basic contact information from your visitors, you can nurture them and — over time — turn them into clients. The best way to do this is to send them email that offers them additional relevant educational content. And you can begin to invite them to take advantage of workshops, consultations or product demos that connect them with members of your staff. Once they make personal contact with your firm, closing the sale becomes much, much easier.

Everywhere, continuously

The success of a content marketing program depends on your ability to build a library of high-quality content over time. It also depends on your content being findable in search engines, so having a solid SEO program in place as you develop blog posts and other material is critical. Keep in mind that relying on people finding your materials through search engines is not enough. You will also want to promote new pieces in social media and, in the case of books or other long-format pieces, press releases and other forms of PR (public relations) may make sense.

But "content marketing" isn't synonymous with "online marketing," nor is it limited to the digital world. Consider all of the places your buyers look for information, and think about how you can use the range of tools available to you to build your reputation and visibility.

Keep your registration forms as short and minimal as possible

Take public speaking. Talks at targeted conferences, associations or other networking events give you a platform to share your issue-related expertise. And today, public speaking can do double duty if it is taped and made available for viewing later.

While much of your content marketing will take place online, be sure to find out where your prospects look for information — both online and offline — and see if you can carve out a space there so that you can build a path to deeper engagement. When clients come searching for answers, you'll be waiting — holding out a helping hand.

As we saw in the last chapter, the most effective brand tools aren't one-and-done efforts, but ongoing commitments. Think of your brand not as a manufactured product but as a crop growing in the daylight of public perception. Like a plant, your brand requires care and cultivation — at every touchpoint of your business. You'll be sowing and harvesting year-round.

Key Takeaways

- Increasing your reputation and visibility is a continuous process.

- The content marketing model boosts your firm's visibility everywhere that buyers might look for relevant information.

- In brand building, there are no shortcuts — it's about continuous and iterative improvement on all fronts.

CASE STUDY

"You Have to Give to Get": Selling to the Management Consulting Industry

As President, CEO, and founder of Evans Incorporated, a consulting firm focused on change management and business transformation, Dr. Sue Evans is a regular consumer of professional services. Her vendors include CPAs, attorneys, financial advisors, consultants for the government/GSA (General Services Administration) sector, contractors and real estate services. If you want Sue to buy your services, there are several things you should know:

The network is paramount
For Sue, when it comes to finding new providers, the network is paramount. She comes into contact with many people through her activity on boards, work with nonprofits and professional organizations, and during the course of professional development and networking events. When she needs a new vendor, she thinks first of those professionals with whom she has fostered relationships. "If I have a specific need and don't have a

personal connection, I'll ask around," says Sue. "I'll say, 'Do you know anyone who does this, specifically?'"

Giving to get

For service providers to have the best chance of winning business from Evans Incorporated, Sue says, "They need to give to get. If a vendor is giving a talk or teaching a seminar, that's the best way to get their information to me, and I appreciate that they're taking valuable time from work to do it." Vendors make themselves visible by offering time to committees, events and workshops.

"It's not enough for vendors to show up at a networking event," says Sue. "Take the time to educate us and we'll get a sense of how you work." When Sue and her peers need a provider, they'll turn first to the sellers they know and trust.

Your website can make or break the deal

Next, Sue researches providers online. At this point, she expects firms to have a strong website that demonstrates their credibility and authority. It should have clear messaging that shows how the firm solves problems. Sue also looks for blogs, whitepapers, research and other content that demonstrates thought leadership. Firms that provide useful information are more likely to win Sue's business.

Selling turn-offs

"I wish I had a Do Not Call list for sales calls," Sue says. Sales callers start off badly by interrupting Sue's already busy day. Then they continue down the wrong path by pushing their services without an established need, doing themselves more harm than good.

By asking for Sue's time without providing anything in return, these sales callers demonstrate why you should "give to get." Professional services firms that offer educational content build credibility with their audience. When that audience needs a provider, they naturally turn to these firms first.

CHAPTER 13
Your Brand Building Plan:
Step by Step

R ebranding your firm takes a lot more than a fresh coat of paint. You have to peek inside your buyers' heads so you can understand how they perceive you and give you the perspective you need to take control of your reputation. You also have to do what it takes to make your firm visible everywhere your target clients look. That way your firm will be top of mind when an opportunity arises. Making these changes is an ongoing, sometimes intensive process, but the payoff is huge: dramatically higher growth and profits. So let's look back at what we've learned and review the steps you need to take in your quest to build a powerful brand.

1. **Think about your business strategy.** What is your vision for the future of your firm? How do you plan to get there? Strong branding builds on the foundation you've laid in your overall business strategy, so it's very important to identify clear goals at the outset.

2. **Define your target clients.** Whom are you looking to serve? Whom are you *best suited* to serve? Trying to be everything to everyone is a recipe for disappointment. Our research indicates that most high growth, high profit professional services firms have a narrowly defined focus. This allows them to create more effective, targeted branding and build a reputation for specialized expertise. But how do you know you've chosen the right target group for *your* firm?

3. **Know your clients.** By now, you know that you need to understand the businesses you serve. Your marketing has to be based on hard data, not hunches. If you research your clients' goals, priorities and points of view, you will be able to speak to their needs in language that resonates with them. Moreover, studying your marketplace can uncover underserved needs or other opportunities. On top of all this, audience research gives you valuable insights into how clients see your firm: your strengths, your weaknesses and the services they associate with your firm. This data both supports your branding efforts and reduces your financial risks — so you won't be expending valuable time and resources on a shot in the dark.

4. **Position your brand.** What's your competitive advantage? Why should businesses in your target audience work with you? As you may recall from Chapter 10, a positioning statement can help you deliver answers internally and externally, and it will serve as a basis for all your marketing work to follow. This is your company's story in four to six sentences. Your story must be succinct, accurate, and meaningful. Though it's an internal document, your positioning statement is a distillation of your brand. It should affirm the qualities of your business that are relevant to everyone who knows it, from staff to prospects to clients. At the same time, it should encompass any aspirational qualities you are striving to embrace. Create a statement that expresses your firm's essence — a unique and grounded assertion of your firm's style, competitive edge and vision.

5. **Develop a messaging architecture.** If your positioning statement is the first pillar of your brand strategy, then your messaging architecture is the second. This document identifies various target audiences — current clients, prospects, potential employees and partners, to name just a few — and turns your brand positioning into specific messages for each. These messages take your brand positioning and emphasize the points of greatest interest and relevance to each audience. Moreover, the messaging architecture identifies each audience's most likely concerns, as well as the best evidence to assuage those concerns and support your message. This is an invaluable resource for sharing your message in a consistent but audience-appropriate way.

Gathering hard data means you won't be spending valuable time and resources on a shot in the dark.

6. **Craft your name, logo and tagline.** Not every firm needs to change its name — for some, it would be a mistake. But new firms, recently merged companies or businesses who want a more memorable or distinctive moniker will want to settle on a name before they move on to other tools and marketing materials. Find a reputable branding firm that can take you through a comprehensive renaming process. Once you know your name, you may need to create a new logo and tagline. This is an exciting step, but remember that these are tools in your branding toolkit, not the brand itself. Without a solid reputation behind it, a logo is an empty symbol. It's easy to forget that your logo and tagline are a means to an end. Don't get caught up in internal squabbles over taste, but focus instead on creating a symbol and tagline that represent your brand in a meaningful way to the audiences who matter.

7. **Assemble your marketing toolkit.** Your branding should be consistent across your firm's materials. Think about your stationery, emails, sales sheets, proposal formats, pitch decks and other everyday tools. This suite of materials should express your firm's brand in a clear, unified way, supporting your messaging and conveying an organized, confident image. Brand guidelines will make it more likely that your visual brand will be applied consistently across the entire spectrum of your marketing materials.

8. **Create a high performance website.** Professional services websites generally come in two flavors. First, you have a branding site — a simple flag planted in the web conveying a firm's basic brand message: who they are, who they serve, and what they do. A branding site is better than nothing, but many high growth firms take advantage of the power of a high performance website. This means building a website that is alive with activity, provides a regular flow of search-optimized educational content and offers a dependable source of expertise and opinion. A high performance website doesn't just plant a flag but provides a place that prospects will want to visit. In such an environment, your content will generate new leads, nurture prospects and continuously enhance your firm's reputation and visibility.

9. **Build out your brand with valuable content.** Reputation and visibility are the twin engines of a successful brand.

It's not much use being visible if no one knows who you are, what you do or how you do it. Likewise, your reputation works hardest for you when it's visible to the entire marketplace you serve. Content marketing offers an ideal way to strengthen your reputation and raise your visibility. When you produce valuable educational content and distribute it for free you demonstrate your expertise, enhance your credibility and create a new way for people to find your firm. Whatever form your content takes — from blog posts to webinars to full-length books — the key is to keep it useful, practical and easy to consume.

10.

Build your brand. Continuously. Too many firms pour a great deal of time and resources into brand development only to lose momentum and turn their focus to more immediate matters. A hard working brand takes hard work — so make sure you commit to the full process, from initial strategy to public launch. That will lay the foundation you need to support future growth and profits.

And if you want content marketing to work, you need to apply the time and resources it demands. Maybe you've read blogs that begin with a New Year's resolution to post weekly … and then trail off after a handful of posts. Don't let that be your firm. To be effective, you need to sustain your output. That's how you build a loyal and eager following. Commit and carry through: your persistence will be evident in your work and create yet another facet of your visible reputation.

A high performance website doesn't just plant a flag but builds a space that prospects will want to visit.

To ensure that your brand development proceeds properly, you must track your progress every step of the way. Metrics you should monitor include search traffic and web visitors, conversions, leads, revenues and employee applications. And that's only a beginning. Along the way you will discover other metrics that are important indicators of your success. Just as your marketing strategy is driven by data, so should your implementation. Only by collecting data can you learn what works and what doesn't, so that you can make adjustments along the way.

A powerful, standout brand is within reach, and it can fundamentally transform your firm. Put yourself in the heads of your buyers, focus on your competitive advantages and produce valuable content for your target clients. It takes careful planning and a lot of work, but the rewards can't be understated. This is how you will move from your position today to a high growth, high profit firm positioned to become a leader.

Key Takeaways

- Conduct your brand development in a logical order, building upon a foundation of business strategy and client research.

- Rethink the way you market your services. Consider producing ongoing educational content. Content marketing builds reputation and visibility at the same time.

- Your website will be the hub of your content marketing strategy.

- Track your progress every step of the way so that you can make the adjustments required to achieve the results you want.

- Monitor key metrics such as search traffic, website visitors, conversions, leads and employee applications.

ADDITIONAL RESOURCES

Books

Professional Services Marketing: Free First Chapter
www.hingemarketing.com/library/article/professional_
services_marketing_book_free_chapter

Online Marketing for Professional Services
www.hingemarketing.com/online-marketing-book

Spiraling Up: How to Create a High Growth, High Value Professional Services Firm
www.hingemarketing.com/spiralingup

Guides

Content Marketing Guide for Professional Services
www.hingemarketing.com/library/article/B2B_content_
marketing_guide_for_professional_services_firms

The Brand Building Guide for Professional Services Firms
www.hingemarketing.com/library/article/the_brand_
building_guide

SEO Guide for Professional Services
www.hingemarketing.com/library/article/seo_guide_for_
professional_services

The Social Media Guide for Professional Services
www.hingemarketing.com/library/article/the-social-media-
guide-for-professional-services

The Lead Generating Website Guide
www.hingemarketing.com/library/article/the_lead_
generating_website_guide

Research Reports

The Hinge Rebranding Kit
www.hingemarketing.com/library/article/the_hinge_
rebranding_kit

How Buyers Buy Technology Services
www.hingemarketing.com/library/article/how_buyers_buy_
technology_services

How Buyers Buy Accounting and Finance Services
www.hingemarketing.com/library/article/how_buyers_buy_
accounting_finance_services

How Buyers Buy Architecture/Engineering/Construction Services
www.hingemarketing.com/library/article/how_buyers_buy_
architecture_engineering_construction_services

How Buyers Buy Management Consulting Services
www.hingemarketing.com/library/article/how_buyers_buy_
management_consulting_services

 What Sales Winners Do Differently
http://info.rainsalestraining.com/free-report-what-sales-
winners-do-differently

Electronic

 The Hinge Professional Services Marketing Blog
www.hingemarketing.com/blog
RSS Feed: http://feeds.feedblitz.com/hingemarketing

 Pivot Newsletter
www.hingemarketing.com/pivot

 Professional Services Executive Forum
www.hingemarketing.com/psef

ABOUT THE AUTHORS

Lee W. Frederiksen, Ph.D., Managing Partner, Hinge

Lee is Managing Partner at Hinge, a premier professional services branding and marketing firm. He brings over 30 years of marketing experience to the firm's clients. Lee is a former tenured professor of psychology at Virginia Tech, author of numerous books and articles, and a successful entrepreneur. He's started and run three high-growth companies, including an $80 million runaway success. Lee has worked with many global brands, including American Express, Time Life, Capital One, Monster.com and Yahoo! He led the research studies that form the basis of this book. He is also a co-author of *Spiraling Up: How to Create a High Growth, High Value Professional Services Firm, Online Marketing for Professional Services* and *Professional Services Marketing, Second Edition.*

lfrederiksen@hingemarketing.com
www.linkedin.com/in/leefrederiksen

Elizabeth Harr, Partner, Hinge

Elizabeth is an accomplished entrepreneur and experienced executive with a background in strategic planning, management, communications and alliance development. Elizabeth co-founded a Microsoft solutions provider company and grew it into a thriving organization that became known for its expertise in Microsoft customer relationship management. Skilled in analytical thinking, process building, change management and brand messaging for successful business growth, Elizabeth has worked with clients in the for-profit, non-profit, and government sectors, helping them map out growth plans using technology adoption. Elizabeth has a Master's degree in International Economics from Columbia University in New York and a B.A. from University of Missouri — Columbia. Elizabeth is active in numerous professional and community service organizations.

eharr@hingemarketing.com
www.linkedin.com/in/eharr

Sylvia Montgomery, CPSM, Senior Partner, Hinge

As a classically-trained marketing executive with a background in graphic design, Sylvia has led marketing teams at several technology and consulting firms — from startups to Fortune 500 firms. Sylvia is a published author and speaker; previously she has served as an adjunct professor at both Trinity College and George Washington University. At Hinge, Sylvia is a senior partner and leads the firm's A/E/C practice, engaging with clients on a daily basis and driving

Hinge's own marketing initiatives. Her on-the-ground experiences provide a real-world dimension to her practical advice. Sylvia is an active member of the Society of Marketing Professional Services (SMPS), DC Chapter. She is a co-author of *Online Marketing for Professional Services*.

smontgomery@hingemarketing.com
www.linkedin.com/in/sylviamontgomery
twitter.com/BrandStrong

Aaron E. Taylor, Senior Partner, Hinge

Aaron is a founding partner at Hinge. In his over 20 years in the industry, he has been an award-winning designer, editor, strategist and writer. Over his career, he's conceived and implemented engaging brand strategies for many professional services firms. Aaron has been published widely in local, regional and national business publications and industry magazines. He is a co-author of *Spiraling Up: How to Create a High Growth, High Value Professional Services Firm* and *Online Marketing for Professional Services*.

ataylor@hingemarketing.com
www.linkedin.com/in/aarontaylorva

ABOUT HINGE

Hinge

Hinge specializes in branding and marketing for professional services firms. Hinge has a reputation for helping firms grow faster and maximize value. Its comprehensive offerings include research and strategy, brand development, award-winning creative, content marketing, lead generating website and marketing outsourcing.

Hinge conducts groundbreaking research on professional services companies, including a group of firms that grow 9X faster and are 50% more profitable yet spend less than average to get new business.

To view Hinge's comprehensive library of research reports, white papers, webinars and articles, please visit www.hingemarketing.com/library.

About Hinge Research Institute

The Hinge Research Institute is committed to conducting innovative research on professional services firms and their respective clients. Its mission is to share that knowledge through research studies, webinars, executive roundtables, whitepapers, articles and books.

Please visit the Institute at www.hingeresearch.com to find additional white papers, podcasts and research reports.

CPSIA information can be obtained
at www.ICGtesting.com
Printed in the USA
BVIC01n0550011113
335197BV00002B

* 9 7 8 0 9 8 2 8 8 1 9 6 5 *